Strategic Planning for Library Managers

Strategic Planning for Library Managers

by Donald E. Riggs

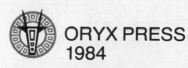

ORYX PRESS
1984

The rare Arabian Oryx is believed to have inspired the myth of the
unicorn. This desert antelope became virtually extinct in the early
1960s. At that time several groups of international conservationists
arranged to have 9 animals sent to the Phoenix Zoo to be the nucleus of
a captive breeding herd. Today the Oryx population is over 400 and
herds have been returned to reserves in Israel, Jordan, and Oman.

Copyright © 1984 by
The Oryx Press
2214 North Central at Encanto
Phoenix, Arizona 85004-1483

Published simultaneously in Canada

Printed and Bound in the United States of America

Library of Congress Cataloging in Publication Data

Riggs, Donald E.
    Strategic planning for library managers.

    Includes index.
    1. Library planning.   2. Library administration.
3. Libraries—Aims and objectives.   I. Title.
Z679.5.R54   1984   025.1   82-73735
ISBN 0-89774-049-1

TABLE OF CONTENTS

PREFACE

The business world has learned that the traditional method of planning is insufficient in our ever-changing and turbulent society. To ensure growth and viability while coping with increasing risk and uncertainty, companies and organizations have been steadily adopting the management techniques of strategic planning. There is nothing new about having to cope with changing circumstances; in fact, this has always been one of the primary responsibilities of library managers. What is different today is the pace at which this change is taking place, the number of directions in which it is occurring, and the increase in its magnitude. An environment is being created which is beset by instability and great uncertainty, one in which libraries need to adopt more flexible strategies in order to survive and thrive.

The theme of strategic thinking and planning has never been more topical than in today's uncertain environment. When recent issues of *Business Week* and the *New York Times* suggest that strategic planners are in great demand, it is certain evidence that strategic thinking is becoming a necessary management function.

Yet the deliberate practice of strategic planning in libraries is regrettably slow in being adopted and rudimentary, despite its wide recognition in the corporate world. Until now, there have been no books devoted exclusively to strategic planning in libraries and fewer than five journal articles written on strategic planning as it pertains to library management. As a result of this void in the library literature, I found myself turning to business and management sources for theoretical and practical applications of strategic planning.

There is hardly a library administrator who would deny the virtues of planning. However, if administrators are to become more than crisis-oriented, they will need to engage in more strategic thinking and planning. The strategic plan itself is not a panacea or a guarantee for success. Some library managers do not want to be committed to a plan because, if there are no written objectives for the library, one can never fail and, if there is no direction, one can never be lost.

Before devising and implementing a strategic plan, library managers must understand the nature of strategic planning and its implications. One of the purposes of this book is to provide general and procedural information on how to go about adopting strategic planning into the library management construct. The book is designed to be used by library directors, associate and assistant directors, department heads, students, and others interested in library management. It should raise the awareness level of librarians to "think and plan strategically."

This book offers a helping hand to managers, so they may better understand and assess where their libraries currently are, where they are going, and what the best ways are to get them to where they want to go. It is a succinct state-of-the-art document on strategic planning, including a descriptive narration of the interrelationships of the various components of a strategic plan and a "how to do it" prescriptive approach for effective implementation. The book provides an introduction to strategic planning; discusses organizing for planning; differentiates among mission, goals, and objectives; underlines the importance of strategy formulation; describes alternatives and contingencies; denotes the roles of policy and resource allocation; rationalizes the involvement of management information systems, the Planning Programming Budgeting System, and the general systems approach; stresses the significance of implementation of the planning process; focuses on planning evaluation and control; and provides concluding observations. In addition to the references given at the end of each chapter, a bibliography of selected resources is provided for the library manager seeking further information on strategic planning.

Strategic Planning for Library Managers

1

SETTING THE STAGE

66Where there is no vision, the people perish. **99**
—Proverbs, 29:18

WHAT IS STRATEGIC PLANNING?

Writers have offered the following definitions of strategic planning:

Strategic planning is the process of deciding on objectives of the organization, on changes in these objectives, on the resources used to attain these objectives, and on the policies that are to govern the acquisition, use, and disposition of these resources.[1]

A continuous process of making present entrepreneurial (risk-taking) decisions systematically and with the greatest knowledge of their futurity; organizing systematically the efforts needed to carry out these decisions; and measuring the results of these decisions against the expectations through organized feedback.[2]

Strategic planning deals primarily with the contrivance of organizational effort directed to the development of organizational purpose, direction, and future generations of products and services, and the design of implementation policies by which the goals and objectives of the organization can be accomplished.[3]

For the purpose of this book, a library's strategic planning process encompasses its mission statement, goals, objectives, strategies, alternatives and contingencies, policies, and resource allocations, and their implementation and evaluation. Particular emphasis is placed on the interrelationship of these components and on the formulation and implementation of strategies. Special attention is also given to the control and evaluation mechanisms necessary to ensure effectiveness in the strategic planning process. One purpose of strategic planning is to determine future areas of activity and decide future courses of action that will result in a high degree of achievement of the library's goals and objectives. In addition, this process provides a set of strategies and policies that contribute a framework for planning and decision making throughout the library. Simply put, the strategic plan gives the goals and objectives of the library and the means by which the library intends to reach them.

While defining strategic planning, it is appropriate to define "strategy." It is derived from "strategos"—meaning a general.[4] In military usage, "strategy" has been long associated with generalship (i.e., determining basic plans of action regarding matters considered to be of critical, even decisive, importance). Regardless of the military overtones, the word "strategic" conveys the kind of planning most needed by today's libraries.

Planning is one of the most important and difficult tasks of modern management. In the early part of this century, organizations were able to enjoy a certain degree of control over their environment. Conditions today, however, are dynamic rather than static. Moreover, Emery notes, they are changing at an even faster rate due to the influence of such factors as economic depression and modern technology. And these changes often occur in a sudden and unpredictable manner similar to turbulence in the atmosphere.[5] Thus, what has emerged to deal with these changes is a "strategic" approach to thinking and planning for the future of rapidly changing organizations.

Strategic planning is not happenstance. It is a complex process requiring much preparation and organization. Strategic planning does not establish a procedure for libraries to eliminate risk; rather, it is a means of recognizing risk and a method for taking advantage of the rewards it might offer. It is more of an art than a science; it is concerned with power and politics. Therefore, it would be folly to expect that a single strategic plan could be developed and implemented for all types of libraries. A small special library will not have a strategic plan identical to the one for a large public library. The organization for strategic planning has to be compatible with and support the goals and objectives of the library. Flexibility has to be built into the strategic planning process in order to accommodate the rapidly changing library environment. The time frame for an effective strategic planning system will normally run from three to five years.

Strategic planning is not a ''bottom-up'' planning process that the library director can delegate to a committee. Since the director is responsible for providing leadership and creating the grand design (including the formulation and execution of strategies) for the library, strategic planning is essentially a ''top-down'' process. It is a people-interactive process; thus, it is important to keep the entire library staff apprised of the strategic planning activities.

One should not perceive strategic planning as an effort to create a ''set in concrete'' plan for the library. Rather, it is a process which is continuously being updated and, in any case, it is not a means for replacing managerial intuition and judgment.

Strategic planning does not focus primarily on daily operational and budgetary issues. It does deal with broad intentions of the library, it serves as a planning process which analyzes future threats and opportunities, and it offers alternative courses of action for the library's consideration.[6] Strategic planning differs from traditional approaches to planning in that, for example, the choice of alternative courses of action for an organization is made only after consideration of strategic decision situations.

WHY STRATEGIC PLANNING?

One of the attributes of the strategic planning process is that it is future-oriented. It encourages simulation of the future; one can project the future on paper and redo it if the results are not desirable. It is important for library managers to determine what they want their libraries to be, say, in five years, then work back in time to determine the strategies they need to reach that goal.

Although modern organizations operate in a dynamic environment, many are dominated by an inherent conservatism. John D. Rockefeller, III, describes the conservatism of organizations in this way:

> An organization is a system, with a logic of its own, and all the weight of tradition and inertia. The deck is stacked in favor of the tried and proven way of doing things and against the taking of risks and striking out in new directions.[7]

Because it looks at organizations in such a systematic manner, strategic planning is most appropriate for use by these conservative organizations. Decisions are made only after thoughtful analysis with all parts of an organization viewed individually and collectively as they interrelate. The process minimizes emotion, guesswork, and intuition and provides a workable solution somewhere between compromise and creativity.

In for-profit organizations, paramount attention must be paid to the "seeds of success and failure." Strategic change must be controlled and directional; bottom lines receive special emphasis. While some tactical mistakes will be tolerated, the master strategy must always be on target. Some years ago, General Robert E. Wood of Sears, Roebuck and Co. observed that "business is like war in one respect, if its grand strategy is correct, any number of tactical errors can be made and yet the enterprise proves successful."[8] Both for-profit and non-profit organizations must have their strategies conceptually well-written and understood, and they must relate directly to overall organizational goals.

The importance of strategic planning in the business world is illustrated by a 1977 survey conducted with chief executive officers of the 500 largest for-profit firms in the United States. One question asked the respondents what their most important responsibility as a chief executive officer was. Planning/strategy ranked first in all companies above management selection/development, capital allocation/profits, policy decisions, and maintaining morale, in that order.[9]

Before getting involved in the strategic planning process, top managers must know what they want from the planning system. Steiner has listed some possible objectives of formal strategic planning. They are not mutually exclusive; some are subsets of others or interrelated. They are not arranged in any order of importance. His 20 suggested objectives are to:

1. Change direction of the company.
2. Accelerate growth and improve profitability.
3. Weed out poor performers among divisions.
4. Flush up strategic issues for top management consideration.
5. Concentrate resources on important things. Guide divisions and research personnel in developing new products. Allocate assets to areas of best potential.
6. Develop better information for top managers to make better decisions.
7. Develop a frame of reference for budgets and short-range operating plans.
8. Develop situation analyses of opportunities and threats to provide better awareness of company's potential in light of its strengths and weaknesses.

9. Develop better internal coordination of activities.
10. Develop better communications.
11. Gain control of operations.
12. Develop a sense of security among managers coming from a better understanding of changing environment and company's ability to adapt to it.
13. Stretch the mind.
14. Train managers.
15. Provide a road map to show where the company is going and how to get there.
16. Set more realistic, demanding yet attainable objectives.
17. Review and audit present activities so as to make proper adjustments and modifications in light of changing environment and company's aims.
18. Provide awareness of changing environment in order to better adapt to it.
19. Pick up the pace of a "tired" company.
20. Because others are doing it.[10]

Based on Carlson's excellent description and justification of strategic planning,[11] the following continuum reveals the benefits realized by moving from traditional planning to strategic planning.

FROM	TO
Random planning	Systematic planning
Reactive decision making	Proactive decision making
Incremental evaluation	Synoptic evaluation
Goal-setting based on operational needs	Goal-setting based on the organization's mission
Isolated decision making	Team decision making
Decision making based on subjective evaluations	Decision making based on objective evaluations as a result of gathering data
Guessing results	Evaluating all possible outcomes

▉LIBRARY MANAGEMENT-RELATED ISSUES▉ ▉AND TRENDS▉

The current period in the history of library management is a complicated one. More than ever before, major external forces are compounding management practices. Shifting of priorities and restructuring of internal programs have brought forth a new era in library planning.

As a consequence of improved services, users have yet greater expectations of their local libraries. They are demanding expansion of existing services, creation of new services, extension of library hours, and enlargement of collections. Better bibliographic access to collections has enabled users to know which libraries hold particular books and journals, and consequently, the users place heavy pressure on local library staff to get materials from other libraries in a shorter turnaround time.

Adequate space to house new services and growing collections is an ongoing challenge for library planners. Unlike the 1960s, there are limited funds to construct new facilities; alternatives and strategies for accommodating space needs have to be developed and assessed. Remote storage and compact shelving are popular alternatives for easing cramped quarters. Reconfigurations of existing space may save funds and provide a "band-aid" solution to the heavy demand in some libraries for more user stations. The growing population has depleted the availability of study carrels and tables in libraries. Frequent complaints are even heard about the lack of parking space adjacent to the local public library.

Technological adaptation could best be described as having a positive impact on library procedures and processes. However, the state of the art of some library technology has evolved at a snail's pace. This exceedingly slow development of particular technological applications (e.g., a workable acquisitions subsystem) has played havoc with planning for a totally automated, integrated library system. Moreover, library managers must try to reconcile all the glittering technology available with the economic realities of library budgets. The following questions deserve answers from library managers who strategically plan on incorporating the role of technology into their library's future:

- When should a library use a home-grown computing system in lieu of purchasing a turnkey system?
- How important is it to have all catalog records in machine-readable format?
- What role will computer reference service play in the technology program?

- Who will train the library staff to use the new technology?
- Will advanced technologies eventually drive the traditional library out of existence?

Austerity and retrenchment are common watchwords throughout the library world. High inflation rates occurring concurrently with reduced annual library budgets have created a double-whammy effect. Competition for funds has intensified within the past few years as city managers, college presidents, corporation leaders, and other budget decision makers take a closer look at library expenditures. Many of them perceive the library as a "bottomless pit" agency/department because, each year, the amount of funds requested by the library grows larger and larger. Planning which library programs to deemphasize and on which existing strengths to build on are key points to consider prior to the redeployment of already scarce resources.

Preventative maintenance of library materials and full-scale conservation measures are being factored into today's library goals and objectives. New funds for conservation of materials will not be easy to justify. Attempts to explain to city officials and state legislators why funds are needed to deacidify materials may fall on deaf ears. It is difficult for budgeteers to comprehend why new funds are needed to preserve materials; they understand requests for new books, but preservation is a phenomenon not yet fully understood.

Changes in staffing patterns and reductions in the work force have created perplexing challenges for library managers. Reductions in precious human resources have left some libraries debilitated. Counteracting a large-scale staff reduction calls for the wisdom of a Solomon and the cunning of a Machiavelli. Effective use of staff during difficult financial times sets forth a rethinking process in personnel planning. A renewed emphasis should be placed on productivity and the quality of the work environment, with the inclusion of strategies for coping with areas often overlooked (e.g., stress and burnout).

Retraining of staff members should be a high priority in any library environment. Continuing education opportunities have to be provided to keep staff members apprised of new developments in their respective specialties. If a new, qualified staff member cannot be employed to oversee implementation of a novel service, then some provision has to be made to train existing staff. Well-designed and well-funded continuing education and staff development programs must be an integral part of a library's planning endeavor.

■WHAT GOOD IS STRATEGIC PLANNING TO■ ■■■■■■■■■■■■■■■■■■■LIBRARIES?■■■■■■■■■■■■■

Libraries are highly complex organizations which are being pressured by societal demands to do progressively more with progressively less. The time has gone when library managers could meet each new day by "planning" on the spur of the moment; today, this "Mickey Finn" approach to management of libraries would be devastating to their well-being, growth, and vitality. An uncertain and muddled environment has intensified the need to plan for the future. Although some library managers may prefer to take an ostrichlike approach to coming change and do what has always been done, it is no longer possible to count on our tradition to maintain momentum in the growth and development of libraries.

In his 1981–82 library annual report, De Gennaro states:

> We have come to an end of an era. Change has overtaken and replaced growth as the dominant driving force in . . . libraries. Librarians, as well as those who use and fund libraries, must come to terms with this new reality. It should be clear to all by now that libraries can no longer afford to do what they tried to do in the past. . . . The forces that have been transforming the library during the last decade are intensifying and accelerating. We will have to move quickly and decisively to take advantage of the opportunities such a climate of change offers. The library can either ride this wave of change or be overwhelmed by it. I believe we can and should ride it.[12]

There is no better time than now for a change in the library manager's mentality. It is an ideal time to begin developing a strategic philosophy to facilitate the library's relationship with its current environment and to provide a better sense of direction and commitment to the library's future.

Davis describes the importance of strategic thinking this way:

> In the placid world of traditional librarianship, strategic thinking was an unnecessary and indeed alien idea connoting conniving in its worst extreme. The library was meant to be carried wherever the satisfaction of the user needs took it. In the turbulent, resource scarce environment of contemporary librarianship, strategic planning becomes indispensable. However, most librarians are simply not practiced in strategic thinking, which requires a shift in mind set. A mind which is used to thinking forward from action to consequences, must begin to focus on "backward analysis" from desirable future outcomes to immediate requirements. Capability to think strategically needs to be developed in most managers; unfortunately, it seldom is.[13]

FEAR OF PLANNING

Since planning involves change, it is sometimes feared because it may mean a disturbance in the status quo, a threat to job security, or a modification in the established way of doing things. Strategic planning is not a panacea for a library's problems, and "bullet biting" and "hard choices" may accompany the process. Administrators who propose change may face resentment—may even run the risk of losing prestige. Perhaps the lack of a plan may satisfy some library managers who do not want to risk taking action and possibly making a mistake.

Reinharth et al. believe that the following are typical planning-related fears:

- It is hard to plan (and I might not do a good job).
- It puts constraints on my actions (if it's not in the plan, I can't do it).
- It forces me to make decisions (and that makes me vulnerable).
- Making a plan provides a yardstick for critique and evaluation (and I might not measure up).
- Planning brings direction and organization out of chaos (and removes a very good excuse).
- Planning brings its own chaos and disruption (when managers resist or choose not to follow the plan).[14]

It is the library director's responsibility to set the stage for the strategic planning process. A positive approach cannot be overemphasized; the immediate benefits and long-range value of planning need to be advocated. For example, the library will gain much knowledge about its strengths, weaknesses, threats, and opportunities during the analysis phase. To ensure that the final planning document is accepted by the staff, it is judicious to keep them informed throughout the different stages of the planning process.

TRANSFORMATIONAL LEADERSHIP

Due to today's internal and external environmental factors, the top-level administrators of libraries are required to be change agents. Even though this book frequently uses the terms "managers" and "management" while discussing strategic planning, it should be understood that the book is geared toward library leaders. As a matter of fact, strategic planning cannot effectively exist in any library setting without strong, creative leadership. The ideal library setting contains managers who are also leaders.

The library leader should not be an inactivist or a reactivist but should be a proactivist who will bring order to chaos and establish strategies for advancing the library into the twenty-first century. While *transactional* leadership deals with day-to-day issues and organizational maintenance, *transformational* leadership deals with planned change.

The spirit of strategic planning and its implications for leadership was presented 350 years ago by Baltasar Jerónimo Gracián y Morales this way:

> Think in anticipation, today for tomorrow, and indeed, for many days. The greatest providence is to have forethought for what comes. What is provided for does not happen by chance, nor is the man who is prepared ever beset by emergencies. One must not, therefore, postpone consideration till the need arises. Consideration should go beforehand. You can, after careful reflection, act to prevent the most calamitous events. The pillow is a silent sibyl, for to sleep over questions before they reach a climax is far better than lying awake over them afterward. Some act and think later—and they think more of excuses than consequences. Others think neither before nor after. The whole of life should be spent thinking about how to find the right course of action to follow. Thought and forethought give counsel both on living and on achieving success.[15]

REFERENCES

1. Robert N. Anthony, *Management Control Systems* (Homewood, IL: Richard D. Irwin, 1965), p. 4.
2. Peter F. Drucker, *Management: Tasks, Responsibilities and Practice* (New York: Harper & Row, 1973), p. 125.
3. William R. King and David I. Cleland, *Strategic Planning and Policy* (New York: Van Nostrand Reinhold, 1978), p. 6.
4. *The Oxford English Dictionary,* Vol. 10 (Oxford: The Clarendon Press, 1933), p. 1087.
5. Fred E. Emery, *Systems Thinking* (New York: Penguin Books, 1969), p. 241.
6. Russell L. Ackoff, *A Concept of Corporate Planning* (New York: John Wiley & Sons, 1970), p. 2.
7. John D. Rockefeller, III, *The Second American Revolution* (New York: Harper & Row, 1973), p. 72.
8. Quoted in A. D. Chandler, *Strategy and Structure: Chapters in the History of the Industrial Enterprise* (Cambridge, MA: M.I.T. Press, 1962), p. 235.
9. Heidrick and Struggles, Inc., *Profile of a Chief Executive Officer* (New York: Heidrick and Struggles, Inc., 1977), p. 4.
10. George A. Steiner, *Strategic Planning: What Every Manager Must Know* (New York: Free Press, 1979), p. 58.

11. Thomas S. Carlson, "Long-Range Strategic Planning: Is It for Everyone?" *Long Range Planning* 11 (June 1978): 54–61.

12. Richard De Gennaro, "Planning Ahead," *Report of the Director of Libraries, University of Pennsylvania, 1981-82* (December 7, 1982): 1–8.

13. Peter Davis, "Libraries at the Turning Point: Issues in Proactive Planning," *Journal of Library Administration* 12 (Summer 1980): 11–24.

14. Leon Reinharth et al., *The Practice of Planning: Strategic, Administrative, and Operational* (New York: Van Nostrand Reinhold Company, 1981), p. 6.

15. Baltasar Jerónimo Gracián y Morales, *The Science of Success and the Art of Prudence;* trans. Lawrence C. Lockley (Santa Clara, CA: University of Santa Clara Press, 1967), p. 45.

CHAPTER

2

ORGANIZING FOR
STRATEGIC PLANNING

66 It is always wise to look ahead, but difficult to look further than you can see. 99
—*Winston S. Churchill*

Despite the inappropriateness of attempting to use any single strategic planning concept to fit all types of libraries, there are a number of trends that have emerged from corporate strategic planning experience that form the premises on which strategic planning for libraries is based. King has concluded that the basic premises are that:

1. Professional planners can facilitate a planning process, but they cannot themselves do the organization's planning.
2. Planning activities should be performed by the managers who will ultimately be responsible for the implementation of the plans.
3. Creative strategic planning involves many different sub-units of the organization and many different varieties of expertise.

4. A "planning organization" must be created to deal with the conception and development of strategic plans. This organization provides the climate and mechanism through which individuals at various levels are provided a greater opportunity to participate in determining the organization's future.
5. Managers must be motivated to spend time on strategic planning through a formalized system and organization approach which also permits their contribution to the planning process to be assessed.
6. The planning process must provide for the development of relevant databases—qualitative as well as quantitative—which facilitate the evaluation of strategic alternatives.
7. An evaluation of future environmental funds, competitive threats, and internal organizational strengths and weaknesses is essential to the strategic planning process.
8. Evolving ideas of organizational participants must be "captured" and incorporated into strategic decision making.
9. The chief executive officer is responsible for developing the planning environment, overseeing the final evaluation and selection of strategic alternatives, and designing an implementation plan to ensure that the strategic choices are put into action.
10. All aspects of strategic planning must be carried on in an integrated and efficient manner.[1]

The "planning to plan" process involves four basic questions:

1. What is the existing situation of the library?
2. What is desired in the future for the library?
3. What might inhibit the desired future of the library?
4. What actions should be taken to achieve the library's goals and objectives?

Organizing for strategic planning includes identifying who in the library is going to participate in the process; determining if outside resource persons (e.g., a consultant) will be used; developing a planning environment; recognizing where the library currently is; analyzing the library's mission, goals, and objectives; identifying which of the existing databases or information systems will be used and what new ones will be created; and projecting which control mechanisms will be developed and implemented. Strategy, policy, contingencies and alternatives, and resource allocations are other important components which will evolve as the planning process unfolds.

PARTICIPANTS IN THE PROCESS

Strategic planning, like other planning techniques, is a human-oriented process. However, unlike other types of planning, strategic planning requires that the library director be highly involved throughout the process. It must be understood that the director cannot handle every aspect of strategic planning alone, but that s/he must effectively use top-level managers, key staff members, and others to ensure that the best organizational thought and creativity are recognized and used. It is crucial for the appropriate persons in the library to have personal involvement in and commitment to the strategic planning process if it is to have long-term effectiveness. Their participation will help offset the antiplanning biases and counter the resistance to change; interactions among the participants will permit necessary adjustments in goals and objectives to be divulged and implemented.

Top management should ask itself searching questions concerning the attitudes within the library toward the strategic planning process, the qualifications of persons who are likely to be given the responsibility for formulation and implementation of strategic plans, the willingness of the library and its present organization to support the planning activity, and effective cooperation among planners and doers in carrying on a multiyear planning program. If those concerns receive positive responses, then one can assume that a good understanding of strategic planning prevails among the various constituencies of the library.

Role of the Library Director

After the library has made the decision to launch into a strategic planning process, it is absolutely essential that the director assume primary responsibility for initiating and overseeing the process. Of course, s/he can and should enlist others to assist with the endeavor, but the overall responsibility cannot be delegated. The director is the linchpin in the development and operations of the strategic planning process. As the director extends him/herself through others, his/her personal support and leadership in planning must be visible to others in the library. For example, if there is a strategic planning committee, the director should chair the committee.

The director must firmly believe in strategic planning and make a commitment of time and energy to it. The success or failure of strategic planning depends, to a large extent, on the attitude of the director—whether s/he believes in it, understands and actively participates in the process, and provides the strong leadership necessary to really benefit from it. If the director introduces strategic planning to the library merely because it is the fashionable thing to do, does not believe or understand it, and thus loses interest in the process, it is bound to fail. According to Hussey, the very first principle of strategic planning is that:

> The chief executive must genuinely desire strategic planning, and he must back his wishes by positive action. Planning must not only be wanted, but it must be seen to be wanted—which means that the chief executive must excite among his senior managers the same desire to practice the planned approach which he himself possesses. He, too, must submit to the same sort of planning discipline as the rest of the company, for nothing is worse for the success of planning than the feeling that this is medicine that the chief reserves for those under him—but which he will never take himself. His personal interest in the planned approach must be as obvious to the company as his edict that this is the philosophy by which the company will be guided.[2]

The director must create an environment for strategic planning that dispels the fears and prejudices of department heads and others. The director needs to know and assess the planning team's predilections toward improvement of the library through strategic planning. S/he can enhance the enthusiasm for strategic planning by discussing the success other organizations have gained from using strategic planning, explaining how library service functions might be done better through strategic planning, describing how strategic planning would be facilitated throughout the library, and revealing how strategic planning would improve the decision-making process.

Role of the Department Head

In a library setting, the department head plays a central role in the strategic planning process. Along with the professional members of the director's office, the department heads constitute the majority of the members of the planning team. A few selected/elected representatives below the department head-level may assist the director with strategic planning. Since strategic planning is essentially a "top-down" process, the department head holds a key position in shaping the future of the library. Many of the goals, objectives, and strategies will most likely be realized through the activities of the departments. Since departments generally have a symbiotic relationship with one another, close cooperation and open communication are required.

Department heads are indispensable in the introduction and implementation of strategic planning. Nevertheless, in many instances, they
have to undergo an attitude change about the planning process. They must
be able to perceive how changes resulting from proper planning can
facilitate constructive interrelationships among the various departments.
Further, they must see the *entire* library picture—how their departments
can benefit from participating in the strategic planning process and also how
they may not necessarily benefit as much as another department in a given
year. Department heads must be committed to strategic planning and be
able to develop a strategic awareness among their department's members.

The essence of strategic planning is determining what direction the
library wants to pursue in the future. Participation of department heads in
the planning process is necessary to ensure that the assumptions upon which
planning is developed are reasonable and that the planning strategies can be
executed. The results of the strategic planning process will likely have their
greatest impact on departmental-level operations, so the activity of department heads in the planning process will provide credibility and realism to a
scenario that would be lacking it without their participation. From the
departmental viewpoint, they can work to reduce overlap and to ensure that
the management's impact throughout the library is integrated, balanced,
and complete.

Role of the Planning Committee

Since strategic planning does not encourage the "bottom-up" approach toward decision making, a lesser emphasis is placed on having
many lower-level library staff participating on the planning committee. The
complexities involved with strategies and tactics preclude any large number
of lower-echelon library staff members serving on the committee because
they lack the time and aptitude for formal planning. However, the committee should include some librarians and clerical staff members, so that a
valuable nonmanagerial perspective is brought to the committee. Also,
these persons can assist with some of the necessary routine work (e.g.,
gathering valuable information, compiling statistics).

Managers must address the formal relationships of roles and the tasks
to be performed in achieving the library's goals and objectives, the grouping of these activities, and the formulation of the appropriate courses of
action. Strategy and the library's formal structure are interdependent.
Bearing these realities in mind, the planning committee should predomi-

nantly comprise library managers, including all department heads and the key personnel in the director's office.

Strategic planning, being a people activity, is a labor-intensive aspect of the library. One of the benefits gleaned from the planning committee is that it allows an orderly forum for key members of the library to "have their day in court." The team concept is further developed through the committee, and its members will have an opportunity to engage in an interchange of ideas that may stimulate creativity. Strategic planning presents an opportunity for the members to look closely at the multidimensional aspects of the library's formal structure. Each department can be critically reviewed in the context of the library's future, and the committee will be in a position to collectively study and strive for conclusions on goals, objectives, strategies, and tactics. Each member brings to the committee invaluable expertise representing the various departments; this is another rationale for composing the committee with care.

The director should chair the committee and, if narrowly focused areas are to be studied during the planning process, s/he may wish to assign project teams or task forces to address them. The project teams or task forces should be created by using members from the planning committee.

Role of Consultants

The use of consultants with certain aspects of the strategic planning process may be worthwhile for some libraries. However, consultants should not do the planning. They can be used to suggest planning procedures, evaluate the feasibility of particular plans, or even suggest some strategies. They could also advise a library on the mechanics of a general fabric for a strategic planning process. Regardless of the valuable assistance consultants can lend to the library in an advisory or facilitating capacity, library management must do the actual planning.

DEVELOPING A PLANNING ENVIRONMENT

After the participants have been identified, the next step is to determine how the planning process will evolve. Questions that should be answered include who will do what, how many financial resources will be allocated for the planning process, and what subcommittees need to be created. The team approach is the best method to use when creating a planning environment. The intent of the strategic planning process must be communicated throughout the library so that surprises about the planning endeavor will be kept to a minimum.

Without the support of its parent organization, efforts by the library to implement the principles of strategic planning may be futile. City governments, academic administrations, school administrations, corporation officers, and state government officials need to acknowledge and support the strategic planning efforts of their library administrators. Ideally, the parent organization will already have a formal strategic plan in effect and, subsequently, the library would be involved as part of the larger plan. However, library administrators must not feel thwarted if their parent organization does not have or intend to have a strategic plan. If the library administration determines that a strategic plan is the proper blueprint for its library, then it should go full speed ahead with developing and implementing such a plan. Nevertheless, the planning technique selected for the library has to be synchronized with the parent organization's plan. The library may use a strategic plan to attack its problems and opportunities while the parent organization is using a planning/management technique, such as Management by Objectives, Zero-Base Budgeting, or the Planning-Programming-Budgeting System. In other words, strategic planning may be part of a larger planning endeavor, since it places primary emphasis on strategy formulation and implementation. Receiving the blessing of the parent organization for the library's use of strategic planning will be an asset in the long run.

Undoubtedly, strategic planning is an intellectual process. It demands the introduction of order and form into the library's planning mechanism even if that mechanism may have been unstructured and a bit freewheeling in the past. More provoking thought has to be directed toward the library's external environment. Outside forces can deal a devastating blow to the mission of the library. Anticipating and detecting changes in the external environment has become a vital part of the library director's responsibility. High rates of inflation, advances in electronic publishing, significant breakthroughs in document delivery, and redirection of funds from the public library to another city agency are some examples of events occurring beyond the walls of the library. Preparing to offset, capitalize on, or cope with external forces bears significantly on the library's decision-making process. The environment established for planning should provide a forum to critically discuss how the outcomes of decisions relate to the library's goals and objectives. Alternative courses of action need to be reviewed prior to any decision being implemented. They should be assessed in a structured framework that will reduce uncoordinated and piecemeal activity. Courses of action derived from the decision-making process should be geared toward optimizing the allocation of library resources. Striving for a workable planning environment cannot be given just passing attention; the effectiveness of strategic planning depends on the planning environment.

Each participant has to show evidence of a commitment to strategic planning. If this commitment is not evident, then that individual should not be involved in the process. The commitment not only involves hard work but a dedication of large amounts of time as well. Library managers cannot wait until they have time available; they must make time for strategic planning. By the library director's active lead in the strategic planning process, the other top-level library managers will realize how the director rates its importance.

Lines of authority and communication have to be established very early in laying the groundwork for planning. Everyone needs to know the chain of command. The library's organizational structure may have to be modified to accommodate strategic planning. If such change is evident, it should be done during the "planning the plan" phase. Managers of the library need to know early if there are to be changes in whom one reports to, reassignments of key personnel, and other redeployment of human resources. Clarifying the procedures for decision making is necessary to ensure a smooth-flowing process. Moreover, the parameters for communicating among the participants will also need to be clearly established at the outset of the planning activity.

Political realities also have to be recognized early in the game. External threats and opportunities have to be considered in light of the approach used by library managers. Strategies and policies should be formulated on the basis of concentrated efforts in areas receiving high priority by city governments and other parent organizations. Particular goals and objectives may have to be delayed a year or two due to unusual political ramifications that are beyond the control of the library's management team. The important caveat to remember is that politics make "strange bedfellows" in any planning scheme.

Honesty and forthrightness are very important attributes that must be reflected throughout the strategic planning process. The concept of "strategy" should not be linked to any connotation of trickery or under-the-table antics. The creators of the library's strategic plan should be mandated to exclude any elements that may border on dishonesty. It is crucial to sustain credibility during and after the planning process.

LIBRARY SELF-ANALYSIS

Strategic planning begins with an objective analysis of the library's current strengths and weaknesses and of how those weaknesses can be corrected. The appraisal must cover every functional area of the library. The results of this self-analysis can then provide a base for pursuing the strategic planning process. Both the library's internal and external environment should undergo systematic surveying for new opportunities and possible threats.

Internal Elements

The internal audit focuses on all major existing operations, services, and activities. Statistics, standards of performance, staff size, staffing patterns, workloads, inputs and outputs, recognized collection development bibliographies, conditions of physical facilities, technological applications, and budget records are some of the many measures one can use to determine the current status of the library. Bellassai identified five areas of analysis to be used while evaluating current resources and services for public libraries. They are:

1. The resources and performance of one's library in comparison with libraries serving similar communities.
2. The effectiveness of specific service outlets in relation to other outlets and to the system as a whole.
3. The proportion of various population subgroups served versus their proportion in the population.
4. The degree to which public library services and levels of service provided meet the needs which can and should be met by public libraries.
5. The amount of resources reasonably available to provide needed services.[3]

The importance of maintaining comprehensive statistics, conducting well-designed surveys, and using reliable performance measures cannot be overemphasized. Data derived from these records/studies will be crucial when the library's goals and objectives are being scrutinized.

External Elements

Analysis of the elements of the external environment will provide critical information for the planning process. External constituencies vary from a tiny number for a small special library to a high figure for the large state library agency. Identifying constituencies is time-consuming for the larger libraries and state library agencies, but all external factors must be fully defined before the planners can determine the best path to pursue in the future.

Managers of all types of libraries need to be aware of new technological developments. Technological change in libraries is one of the most difficult areas to plan for, to accommodate, and to make accurate predictions about. Moreover, new technologies are requiring library managers to rethink their existing organizations and services; the shrinking budgets and the introduction of sophisticated technologies require better planning in redeployment of scarce resources while dealing successfully with a changing library environment. It is predicted that, during the next decade, technological advances will affect library service more than one can imagine. The burden is on library leaders to put technology into the right perspective. They are too often on the wrong end of the innovation spectrum when technology is involved; they spend too much time worrying about technology or buffering their library from its undesirable and unintended consequences.

Persons responsible for the future of libraries should be aware of the prospective competing forces that may replace part or all of the library's functions. Information vendors have made substantial progress during the past dozen years, and their momentum is having a ''snowballing'' effect on the users of information. Libraries must have a clear definition of what their central purpose is and how this raison d'etre differs from or complements what information brokers are doing. For example, had the railroads realized several decades ago that the business they were in was the broader business of transportation and not only the narrower railroad freight business, they would have realized the inroads that other competitors were making in their business of transportation. The point is that libraries must recognize the competing forces in the external environment and plan with a full range of services in mind. New services may require a different set of skills and resources in order for libraries to compete successfully with external forces and to thrive in the future.

Total Elements

The internal and external elements of the library's environment are interrelated. This spider's-web relationship is invaluable to keep in mind during the complete analysis of a library. Elements uncovered during the analysis will include key trends, forces, and phenomena that may have a potential impact on the formulation and implementation of strategies.

Steiner describes the complete analysis of an organization by using the WOTS UP acronym. WOTS UP stands for weaknesses, opportunities, threats, and strengths underlying planning. He goes on to imply that some corporations begin strategic planning with a WOTS UP analysis.[4] A library's planning team should give consideration to WOTS UP analysis during its "total entity" look at the library's current and future status. The "total entity" approach furnishes the necessary forum to dissect the library in such a manner that the self-analysis will be practical and useful in the strategic planning process. Looking at the total library organization is a complex task, and it calls for excursions into creative and unconventional thought patterns (e.g., brainstorming) on the part of those involved.

IDENTIFYING POLICIES

Library policies establish the limits, ranging from very broad to very narrow, within which certain types of action may be taken. For example, a state library agency may proclaim "It is our policy to provide service to the disadvantaged library user." Normally, policy is (1) a guideline for carrying out actions, (2) a procedure for preventing errors from recurring, (3) a means for coordinating and controlling the decision-making process, and (4) an ongoing procedure to help library management solve specific problems.

While getting ready for strategic planning, all policies need to be collected and collated according to specific areas of the library. The planning team must be prepared to accept the fact that former understandings and established perimeters that have served as guides to the library's thinking and action will be in a constant state of flux throughout the strategic planning activity. It is recommended that an easy-to-update manual of policies be available for each member of the planning team (policy formulation will be addressed in a later chapter).

INFORMATION FOR PLANNING

One of the most vital aspects of any planning endeavor is the proper collection, analysis, and use of information. The existence of real problems, opportunities, strengths, and weaknesses will only be detected by a well-developed information system. This system must be put in place during the early stages of the planning process and must be more formal than informal. Moreover, the system's primary attributes must be timeliness and comprehensiveness.

Information can come from patron, staff, and community surveys; statistics maintained by governmental agencies, libraries, and the libraries' parent organizations; and community profiles. The prerequisite to proper use of information is careful analysis and synthesis of the data collected.

The information database will be referred to many times during the course of strategic planning. Past, as well as current, performance of the library's departments should be reflected in the database. To ensure consistency, standardized performance measure forms have to be used while collecting performance data. McClure emphasizes that library planners must do a better job in:

> Marshalling the vast array of information sources necessary to resolve complex planning decisions. . . . Planning approaches must include administrative strategies to improve organizational information handling ability, develop programs of information resources management, and increase the staff's ability to manage, coordinate, and integrate information into the planning process. Planning methodologies and planners must address this need.[5]

THE PLANNING MANUAL

At the outset of the strategic planning process, library managers are encouraged to begin writing a planning manual. This manual may be referred to as the "plan to plan" or the planning guide. The manual will continue to evolve throughout the entire planning process. Only a small amount of specific information can be included in the manual at the initial phase of the planning process. As the plan unfolds, the manual eventually will become the official document for the library's strategic plan. Some items which may be included in the manual are:

- An introductory statement by the library director. This statement should indicate the director's commitment to strategic planning.

- Names and positions of the planning team.
- Information and data resources, as well as the methodology of information/data collection.
- An overview of the strategic planning process and the planning environment.
- Brief statements on the library's self-analysis conclusions.
- Mission, goals, objectives, strategies, tactics, and policies; major decisions and implementation plans.
- Resource allocations.
- Brief statements on the management information system.
- Evaluation and control mechanisms.
- A glossary of terms.
- Other pertinent information, depending on a particular library's requirement.

ORGANIZATIONAL CHANGE

While organizing for strategic planning, library managers have to be cognizant of the fact that the planning process will result in several changes. It is the responsibility of the managers to anticipate these changes and make the necessary provisions to accommodate the modifications and innovations. The delivery of quality library service must be sustained, and departmental productivity must be enhanced even though much time and attention is being devoted to the planning activity.

Managers will undergo a change in attitude when they begin thinking strategically about their departments, areas of responsibility, and the total library system. Future targets of opportunities will be a major part of their managerial thinking. Their problem-solving approach will be transformed from that of "reacting, relying on past experience, low risk," to "anticipating, finding new approaches, higher risk." Some managers within the library may perceive some of the changes in a negative view, while others will be very enthusiastic about them. The trick to a successful strategic planning experience is to use an educational approach. Well-planned training sessions, workshops, and some informal, freewheeling sessions are suggested as ways for getting started on the right foot toward a meaningful, positive change in the library's planning process.

PITFALLS TO AVOID

At the beginning of the strategic planning endeavor, it is very easy to get off to a bad start for many reasons. One reason may be that one cannot conceptualize the strategic planning process in its entirety. Naturally, all library managers involved in strategic planning would prefer a positive, rewarding experience. They want to avoid the perils that may result from a bad experience or simply a misunderstanding. To possibly avoid these potential dangers, Steiner devised the following list of 50 common pitfalls in strategic planning, which, even though primarily directed toward for-profit organizations, are also applicable to libraries.

A. Pitfalls in Getting Started
1. Top management's assumption that it can delegate the planning function to a planner.
2. Rejecting planning because there has been success without it.
3. Rejecting formal planning because the system failed in the past to foresee a critical problem and/or did not result in substantive decisions that satisfied top management.
4. Assuming that the present body of knowledge about planning is insufficient to guide fruitful comprehensive planning.
5. Assuming that a company cannot develop effective long-range planning in a way appropriate to its resources and needs.
6. Assuming that comprehensive corporate planning can be introduced into a company and overnight miraculous results will appear.
7. Thinking that a successful corporate plan can be moved from one company to another without change and with equal success.
8. Assuming that a formal system can be introduced into a company without a careful and perhaps "agonizing reappraisal" of current managerial practices and decision-making processes.
9. Ignoring the power structure of a company in organizing the planning process.
10. Failure to develop a clear understanding of the long-range planning procedure before the process is actually undertaken.
11. Failure to create a climate in the company which is congenial and not resistant to planning.
12. Failure to locate the corporate planner at a high enough level in the managerial hierarchy.

Reprinted with permission of The Free Press (a division of Macmillan Publishing Co., Inc.) from *Strategic Planning: What Every Manager Must Know* by George A. Steiner. © The Free Press, 1979.

13. Failure to make sure that the planning staff has the necessary qualities of leadership, technical expertise, and personality to properly discharge its responsibilities in making the planning system effective.

B. Pitfalls Related to a Misunderstanding of the Nature of Strategic Planning

14. Forgetting that planning is a political, a social, and an organizational, as well as a rational process.
15. Assuming that corporate comprehensive planning is something separate from the entire management process.
16. Failure to make sure that top management and major line officers really understand the nature of long-range planning and what it will accomplish for them and the company.
17. Failing to understand that systematic formal planning and intuitive (opportunistic, or entrepreneurial) planning are complementary.
18. Assuming that plans can be made by staff planners for line managers to implement.
19. Ignoring the fact that planning is and should be a learning process.
20. Assuming that planning is easy.
21. Assuming that planning is hard.
22. Assuming that long-range planning can get a company out of a current crisis.
23. Assuming that long-range planning is only strategic planning, or just planning for a major product, or simply looking ahead at likely development of present product. (In other words, failing to see that comprehensive planning is an integrated managerial system.)

C. Pitfalls in Doing Strategic Planning (Managerial Involvement)

24. Top management becomes so engrossed in current problems that it spends insufficient time on long-range planning, and the process becomes discredited among other managers and staff.
25. Long-range planning becomes unpopular because top management spends so much time on long-range problems that it ignores short-range problems.
26. Failure to assume the necessary involvement in the planning process of major line personnel.

27. Too much centralization of long-range planning in the central headquarters so that divisions feel little responsibility for developing effective plans.

D. Pitfalls in Doing Strategic Planning (The Process of Planning)

28. Failure to develop company goals suitable as a basis for formulating long-range plans.
29. Assuming that equal weight should be given to all elements of planning (i.e., that the same emphasis should be placed on strategic as on tactical planning, or that the same emphasis should be accorded to major functional plans).
30. Injecting so much formality into the system that it lacks flexibility, looseness, and simplicity, and restrains creativity.
31. Failure to make realistic plans (e.g., due to overoptimism and/or over-cautiousness).
32. Extrapolating rather than rethinking the entire process in each cycle (i.e., if plans are made for 1984 through 1989, adding 1990 in the 1985 cycle rather than redoing all plans from 1985 to 1989).
33. Developing such a reverence for numbers that irreverence for intuition and value judgments predominates the thinking going into planning.
34. Seeking precision of numbers throughout the planning horizon.
35. Assuming that older methods to choose from among alternatives should be discarded in favor of new techniques.
36. Assuming that new quantitative techniques are not as useful as advertised.
37. Doing long-range planning periodically and forgetting it in between cycles.

E. Pitfalls in Doing Strategic Planning (Creditability of Results)

38. Failure to develop planning capabilities in major operating units.
39. Failure of top management and/or the planning staff, to give departments and divisions sufficient information and guidance (e.g., top management interests, environmental projections, etc.).
40. Attempting to do too much in too short a time.
41. Failure to secure that minimum of system and information to make the process and its results creditable and useful.

F. Pitfalls in Using Strategic Plans

42. Failure of top management to review with departmental and divisional heads the long-range plans which they have developed.

43. Forgetting that the fundamental purpose of the exercise is to make better current decisions.
44. Assuming that plans once made are in the nature of blueprints and should be followed rigorously until changed in the next planning cycle.
45. Top management's consistently rejecting the formal planning mechanism by making intuitive decisions which conflict with the formal plans.
46. Assuming that because plans must result in current decisions it is the short run that counts and planning efforts as well as evaluations of results should concentrate on the short run.
47. Failing to use plans as standards for measuring managerial performance.
48. Forgetting to apply a cost-benefit analysis to the system to make sure advantages are greater than costs.
49. Failing to encourage managers to do good long-range planning by basing reward solely on short-range performance measures.
50. Failing to exploit the fact that formal planning is a managerial process which can be used to improve managerial capabilities throughout a company.[6]

REFERENCES

1. William R. King, "Strategic Planning for Public Service Institutions: What Can Be Learned from Business?" *Journal of Library Administration* 2 (Summer, Fall, Winter, 1981): 44–45.

2. David E. Hussey, *Introducing Corporate Planning,* 2nd Edition (New York: Pergamon Press, 1979), p. 18.

3. Marcia C. Bellassai, "Public Library Planning and the ALA/PLA Process: What's In It for Your Library?" *Journal of Library Administration* 2 (Summer, Fall, Winter, 1981): 86.

4. George A. Steiner, *Strategic Planning: What Every Manager Must Know* (New York: Free Press, 1979), pp. 142–44.

5. Charles R. McClure, "Planning for Library Services: Lessons and Opportunities," *Journal of Library Administration* 2 (Summer, Fall, Winter, 1981): 22.

6. Steiner, pp. 290–93.

3

MISSION, GOALS, AND OBJECTIVES

❝ "Cheshire," Alice asked, "Would you please tell me which way I ought to go from here?" "That depends on where you want to get to," said the cat. ❞
—Lewis Carroll, Alice in Wonderland

After the planning team has become organized, the first step in the strategic planning process is to review the library's mission, goals, and objectives. Since strategic planning focuses on future directions for the library, all of the goals and objectives must be carefully reviewed, revised, and made current. The level of specificity becomes greater as one moves from the mission statement to the goals and objectives.

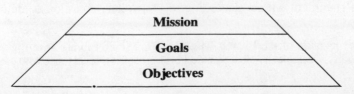

MISSION

Mission statements are generally written in an abstract manner. They express the raison d'etre of the library in broad terms. However, the mission of the library has to be stated in such a way that it reveals the long-term vision of what the library intends to do while, at the same time, giving the reason for its existence. A stated mission should never be considered "carved in stone." It should encourage creative growth and give the library meaning and legitimacy. It makes easier the task of identifying opportunities and threats, and it enables the library managers to move forward in a systematic manner.

In the corporate world, the question asked by companies when reviewing their mission is "What is the company's business?" Drucker feels that to neglect this question is a prime reason for an organization's failure. He says that:

> A business is not defined by the company's name, statutes, or articles of incorporation. It is defined by the want the customer satisfies when he buys a product or a service. To satisfy the customer is the mission and purpose of every business. The question "What is our business?" can therefore, be answered only by looking at the business from the outside, from the point of view of customer and market. What the customer sees, thinks, believes, and wants, at any given time, must be accepted by management as an objective fact. The customer only wants to know what the product or service will do for him tomorrow. All he is interested in is his own values, his own wants, his own reality. For this reason alone, any serious attempt to state "What our business is" must start with the customer, his realities, his situation, his behavior, his expectations, and his values.[1]

Libraries can follow Drucker's advice by asking "What is the library's business?" The service aspect will quickly come to mind when this question is examined. However, Drucker's question deals primarily with an assessment of the current status of the library. Another good question to ask is "What *will be* the library's business?" This question forces the library management to look to the future and to think about possible changes that may better satisfy the needs of the users.

Writing a mission statement is an individual library issue; there is no one statement that could be applied to all types of libraries. Following is a mission statement which, according to Detweiler, consciously delineates service:

> The mission of the Everett [Washington] Public Library is to make readily available the most wanted library materials to all those who use

the library, to serve as an access point for any needed information and to provide the services at an affordable cost.[2]

Another example of a mission statement is:

To provide bibliographical, physical, and intellectual access to recorded knowledge and information consistent with the present and anticipated teaching and research responsibilities and social concerns of Cornell [University].[3]

A library's mission has to be in congruence with its parent organization's mission. For example, a university library's mission cannot contain aspects that are diametrically opposite to those of the university itself. Following is an example of a mission statement for Arizona State University, parent institution of the Arizona State University Libraries:

As a publicly assisted institution, the mission of Arizona State University is:

—To provide broad opportunity for participation in the creation, dissemination and use of knowledge and artistic expression,

—To stimulate individual achievement of highest intellectual and cultural levels, and

—To provide facilitative professional and research services in support of individuals and organizations,

in order to enhance the State of Arizona's return on its investment in human resources for the purpose of supporting social, economic, scientific, technological and cultural advancement.

In pursuit of its mission, Arizona State University should continue to develop as a major research university with special emphasis on programs needed in the State's major urban area, to become competitive with the best public universities in the nation, and to recognize a special commitment to affirmative action and quality of student life.[4]

To illustrate how a library's mission statement relates to the parent organization's mission, here is the mission statement for the Arizona State University Libraries:

The primary responsibility of the Arizona State University Libraries is the support of the current and anticipated instructional, research, and service programs of the University. This responsibility entails the procurement, organization, maintenance, and availability of library resources necessary for these programs.[5]

All employees should understand their library's mission. This understanding can be enhanced by having open discussions about the mission statement during its periodic review. The importance of the mission statement is not to be discounted, since all goals, objectives, strategies, and policies are predetermined by the organization's mission.

GOALS

The words "goals" and "objectives" are used interchangeably in the corporate world. However, many nonprofit organizations use "goal" as an umbrella term, to be followed by the more narrowly defined objectives. For the purpose of this book, goals will precede objectives, with goals being based on the mission statement. Chen provides the following comprehensive definition of a goal:

> A goal is a broad or general statement of desired or intended accomplishment. Its scope is broad and unspecific, and it is usually long-term in nature (two to five years). It may also describe the function which a department serves. For example, the goals of a reference department may be: "To provide quality information services to users." Note that broad terms, such as *quality information services,* do not offer any measurable conditions, which would be the role of an *objective* rather than a *goal*. The statement of goals simply allows a view of the forest instead of the trees.[6]

Goals must be capable of being converted into specific, measurable objectives. As an unknown author noted, "If you don't know where you are going, any road will get you there." Goals give direction and set forth long-run library priorities. They make up an extremely important part of the strategic planning process as they specify declarations of the library's purpose.

Three types of goals have been identified for public libraries, with applicability to other types of libraries as well. They are:

A. *Service goals,* with objectives that specify the types and levels of service to be provided and the individuals to be served by the library. If special target groups were identified by surveys, specific objectives defining the types and targeted levels of services to be provided of these groups may be included.

B. *Resource management goals,* which support the service goals established by the planning committee. Primarily concerned with operations at the system and branch levels, these goals and objectives relate to collections, staff, and facilities, and may include:

1. Collections
    a. Relevance to user groups.
    b. Ratios of print and non-print materials.
    c. Acquisitions (scope, duplication, and timeliness).
    d. Materials availability (delivery time).
    e. Average use per item (turnover rate).
    f. Weeding targets.
2. Staff
    a. Productivity.
    b. Training.
    c. Communication.
    d. Employment conditions.
3. Facilities
    a. Accessibility.
    b. Adequacy.
    c. Utilization.
    d. Maintenance.
    e. Automation.
C. *Administrative or directional goals,* which include developments in library organization, coordination of divisions, cooperative activities, relationships with other governmental units, and future planning activities. For the most part, specific objectives in this category are qualitative rather than quantitative, and serve primarily to verbalize the commitment of library administrators to a course of action to implement service goals and meet community responsibilities.[7]

As an example of how overarching, conceptual library goals may be written, the following are the goals for the Arizona State University Libraries:

A. Collections
    1. To select, acquire, and maintain resource material for supporting instructional, research, and service functions of the University.
    2. To develop and promote a quality program of resource sharing and alternative access in order to serve the needs of local users and to support the cooperation efforts of libraries in general.
    3. To develop policies and procedures that will ensure the preservation and security of the Libraries' collections.

B. Services
   1. To promote understanding of the Libraries' research capabilities and to encourage the use of their resources and services.
   2. To optimize bibliographic control of the Libraries' collections.
   3. To enhance assistance to users in identifying and locating recorded information.
   4. To strengthen accessibility to the University's library resources.
   5. To facilitate access to materials other than those in the University Libraries' collections.
C. Facilities
   1. To provide space, equipment, and technology which will ensure operational efficiency, improve collection preservation, and respond to changing needs of users and staff.
D. Personnel
   1. To maintain a comprehensive personnel program designed to attract, develop, and retain sufficient number of qualified staff capable of meeting the needs of the Libraries' users.
E. Finance
   1. To solicit and secure that financial support necessary for the continuation and expansion of operations of the Libraries.
   2. To administer the Libraries' budget and promote optimum use of their financial resources.
F. Administration
   1. To lend leadership in the promotion, interpretation, and support of the Libraries through the development of constructive relationships with the University administration, academic departments, students, and the Libraries' public in general.
   2. To plan and develop an efficient and effective library system.
   3. To encourage active communication at all levels throughout the Libraries.[8]

The above six areas are not in any priority order. In addition to these overall goals for the Libraries, each department has its own goals.

Goals must stem from the library staff; they cannot be written in isolation or by one person. In addition to consulting with and involving the staff, outside constituents such as the library's governing board or parent organization must be kept informed of the changes in and development of goals. Goals should never be beyond the realm of reality.

The strategic planning team also has to consider the cause-effect relationship between the library's overall goals and the operational goals/objectives of each individual department. The importance of strategic planning becomes apparent only in the light of the interrelated characteristics among the different departments and how their interdependence ties in with the mission, goals, objectives, strategies, and policies. Goals provide a definitive direction and serve as the planning skeleton for integrating the efforts of all library departments into a total library effort. Goodwill needs to prevail throughout the goal-setting process. Hussey underscores the importance of having esprit de corps and a clear definition of what is to be done during the goal setting endeavor:

> [Goals] . . . may be regarded, when used in appropriate manner, as the beacon which on a dark night welcomes the fishing fleet into the safety of the harbor; used badly they can become the sweet singing sirens which lure the unsuspecting vessel to founder on the rocks of disaster.[9]

OBJECTIVES

Unlike goals, objectives are specific and are stated in terms of a particular result that will be accomplished by a specified date. Objectives are more internally focused than goals, and they imply a resource commitment, challenging library management to use necessary resources in order to achieve the desired results. They are purposeful, short-termed, consistent with goals, linked to other objectives, precise, measurable, verifiable, understandable, and flexible. Objectives could be described as the landmarks and milestones which mark the path toward the library's goal(s).

While formulating objectives for the library's departments, Hardy recommends that the following questions be asked:

1. Is the objective designed to contribute directly to the achievement of one or more of the library's goals?
2. Is the objective feasible in light of internal and external constraints?
3. Is the objective measurable? Are the results observable?
4. Were those who are accountable for achievement involved in setting the objectives?
5. Were those who will be affected by the objective involved in the process of formulation?
6. Does the objective have a challenging quality?
7. If the objective involves other departments, was it established collaboratively?[10]

The objective-setting process encompasses four stages: preliminary, tentative, revised, and final. It is prudent for library managers to be cognizant of the intricacies associated with each stage. They should check to see if objectives selected can be achieved simultaneously in a given year of a multiyear plan. For each year, under each prioritized goal, the objectives should be ranked in priority order. By ranking the objectives, priorities for action are established. These objectives need to be scrutinized during each year to determine if new conditions have dictated a re-ranking of them. For example, one objective may have to be broken into two or more smaller objectives in order to be attainable. Possibly, the revised objectives may fall under a new goal. A library's strategy formulation process is not complete until the objectives have been verified with the strategies. If an objective has been assessed as unachievable, it will have to be modified or dropped for a new one. Finding the proper balance between objectives and strategy makes up the final stage of the objective-setting process. Following are two examples of goals that are supported by measurable objectives:

Goal: To make the library collections more relevant to the needs of users.

Objective: To increase to 15 percent the proportion of the total budget spent on materials.

Objective: To increase the turnover rate of materials to three average circulations per item per year by 1984.

Objective: To spend 20 percent of the annual materials budget for subscriptions.

Objective: To increase non-print holdings to 10 percent of the total collection by the end of a five-year period.

Objective: To maintain an annual weeding rate of at least five percent.

Objective: To increase the proportion of total new acquisitions devoted to popular in-demand materials.[11]

Goal: To implement an integrated online (computer) library system over a four-year period.

Objective: To begin a circulation control subsystem by 1984.

Objective: To introduce an online public access catalog by 1985.

Objective: To have in effect an acquisitions subsystem by 1986.

Objective: To bring up a serials control component in 1987.

Establishing objectives is one of the most critical areas in the strategic planning process. It is paramount to have members of each library department address in detail the objectives for the department. Objectives constitute the targets that strategy is intended to reach.

REFERENCES

1. Peter F. Drucker, *Management: Tasks, Responsibilities, Practices* (New York: Harper & Row, 1974), pp. 79–80.
2. Mary Jo Detweiler, "Planning: More Than Process," *Library Journal* 108 (January 1, 1983): 25.
3. Cornell University, "Statement of Mission," Cornell University Libraries (December 19, 1972). Mimeograph.
4. Arizona State University, An Informal Planning Document (January 1983): 21. Mimeograph.
5. Donald E. Riggs, *Arizona State University Libraries Annual Report, July 1, 1981–June 30, 1982* (July 30, 1982): 2.
6. Ching-chih Chen, *Zero-Base Budgeting in Library Management: A Manual for Librarians* (Phoenix, AZ: Oryx Press, 1980), p. 24.
7. Vernon E. Palmour et al., *A Planning Process for Public Libraries* (Chicago: American Library Association, 1980), p. 58.
8. Riggs, pp. 4–6.
9. David E. Hussey, *Introducing Corporate Planning*, 2nd Edition (New York: Pergamon Press, 1979), p. 34.
10. James M. Hardy, *Corporate Planning for Nonprofit Organizations* (New York: Association Press, 1972), p. 65.
11. Palmour, p. 250.

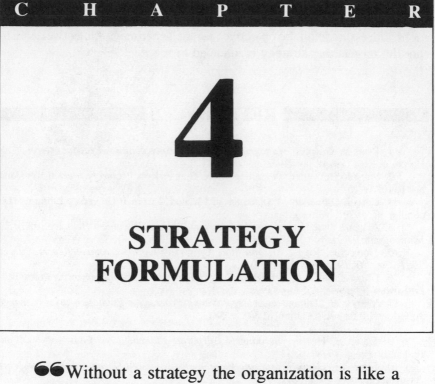

CHAPTER

4

STRATEGY FORMULATION

66 Without a strategy the organization is like a ship without a rudder, going around in circles. It's like a tramp; it has no place to go. 99
—*Joel Ross and Michael Kami*

After the mission, goals, and objectives of the library have been established, the next step is to formulate program strategies. Through strategies, the mission, goals, and objectives will be realized. There is no more important part in the strategic planning process than actually dealing with strategies.

While policies are seen as broad guides to actions, strategies are seen as specific major actions or patterns of action for achieving goals and objectives. Strategies are normally well-conceived and well-planned, but they can also emerge from ad hoc situations. A strategy entails an explanation of what means will be used to obtain its goals and objectives. Therefore, it should be understood that, to take any course of action, a library will have to use some of its resources. Perceived opportunities and threats in the existing or foreseeable library environment will, therefore, have a mean-ingful impact on decisions made for deploying resources.

The responsibility of strategy formulation has traditionally rested with top management. However, the task of strategy development reaches beyond the scope of the library director and his/her assistants, extending to department heads, who are expected to interpret, clarify, and refine the library's existing and proposed strategies. This means that a substantial amount of managerial discretion lies outside of the director's office. Nevertheless, the director cannot delegate the overall responsibility for developing strategies. Installing purpose in place of improvisation and planned progress in place of organization drift are, first and foremost, the responsibilities of the director. Dynamic leadership is necessary to ensure that the library's strategies possess a magnetic and cohesive quality. The process of strategy formulation is never-ending; the director's role is to set the stage for understanding strategy formation, involve line and staff personnel in the process, motivate all those working with strategy develop-ment, mediate conflicts, and ensure an orderly integration of changes into the library system.

Strategy is a major key to the library's success. Every strategy should be consciously designed and regularly assessed. The library's leadership must fully understand that its strategy essentially revolves around a proac-tive stance. Strategy cannot take place as a matter of course, and it should not cause the library to be responding/reacting and being constantly on the defensive.

Strategies can be of several different types. Every library has a strategy, however insignificant or unconscious it may be. The strategy may be explicit, or it may have been deduced from the library's action and operating patterns. Since strategy formation is more of an art than a science, there is no one best way to develop a strategy. A strategy generally represents a practical choice—it will enable a library to move from where it is today (as indicated by the self-study) to where it wants to go in the future (based on goals and objectives). Strategy should be perceived as an evalua-tion of the alternatives open to the library and a selection of what appears to be the best course(s) of action to pursue.

It is significant to distinguish strategy itself from the operational activities (tactics) used to carry out strategies. While strategy is the overall design within which tactical moves are made, tactics are plans that extend for one year or less. Tactics are important measures in getting things done at the operational level. Hutchinson differentiates between strategies and tactics this way:

"In a military sense, strategy involves the planning and direction of projects or campaigns, while tactics deal with the operational aspects of moving or handling forces or units. . . . Strategic decisions encompass the broad development of broad directions and comprehensive plans needed to move an organization toward the achievement of its principal goals. Tactics are the specific means by which these goals can be attained. . . . Wars are fought according to strategic plans, while battles or skirmishes involve tactical plans."[1]

Whereas strategies tend to be developed for the entire library system, tactics are developed primarily for a particular library function or department. Tactics involve more objectivity than strategies do in the decision-making process. Also, less uncertainty and risk are associated with tactics.

MISTAKES TO AVOID

While delineating strategy, one should take care to avoid some common mistakes. Such mistakes, according to Hofer, include confusing goals and objectives with strategies, stating only the manner in which strategy will change in the future, making an incomplete description of the strategy components, failing to see interrelationships involved at the conceptual and operational levels, failing to distinguish between the different types of strategies, looking only for explicit strategy statements, and forgetting to consider actions taken in the past in strategy formulation.[2]

INTEGRATING STRATEGY WITH ORGANIZATIONAL DESIGN

Each library will have unique strategies designed to match the library's organizational construct. Strategy has to be developed in such a way that it facilitates the management process of the library. Strategy becomes integrative when it functions in unison with the library's structure, enabling the library to exploit library opportunities available for improvement in services and operations. Accelerating changes in economic, political, social, and technological forces have to be accommodated in the library's strategy and organizational design.

External Environment

The turbulent external environment beyond the library's jurisdiction is difficult to anticipate and plan for with any high degree of certainty. For example, the annual increase in the cost of library materials is beyond the control of any library. Decisions on the library's budget are made by administrators outside of the library's organizational structure. Even the efficiency aspect of borrowing books and journal articles from other libraries is determined by someone other than the local library. These external forces and constituencies are extremely important variables to be considered while developing strategy. Finally, the library's design has to be constructed in such a fashion to cope effectively and strategically with the forces, threats, problems, and opportunities in the external environment.

Internal Environment

Control of the internal library environment is more feasible than that of the external environment. For example, library management can facilitate strategy by dividing the work to be done. If a library wants to enhance its automation and systems programs, it may choose to employ an assistant director to lend leadership to these two areas. A strategy for better utilization of staff may be implemented by merging certain similar units under a single department head. For example, placing circulation, reserves, current periodical service, microforms, and interlibrary loan under the head of access services may help facilitate more efficient use of staff among the different areas during low- and high-activity periods. Such examples show ways that the library can exercise control over its own environment. The span of control used by library managers may have to be truncated or expanded, however, depending upon particular strategy. To allow more time for planning and strategy implementation, it may be necessary for the director to limit the number of persons reporting to him/her. The internal environment of the library can usually be described as one of the following three types:

1. *Stable*. The library is confronted with familiar problems and opportunities. There is an infrequent need for change in the stable environment. This environment fits the bureaucratic organization with risk aversion, centralization, programmed activity, and tight control.
2. *Flexible (through regulation)*. Under this type of environment, the library is also confronted with familiar problems and opportunities,

but there is a frequent need for change. Regulated flexibility has some decentralization, separate planning, and limited participation in planning.

3. *Adaptive*. The library tends to be confronted with unprecedented problems and opportunities. The adaptive situation fits the library that has more risk-taking strategies, more participation in decision-making activities and planning and control, with emphasis on objectives and results.[3]

It should be understood that each library will not fit exactly into one of these environmental types. These examples simply provide a basis for designing the library's structure for implementing a strategy.

Strategic planners must give careful consideration to the library's strategy in relation to its organizational structure. The two must be compatible.

GOALS FOR CHANGE

Why are goals set during the strategic planning process? Because they serve to break down psychological hang-ups within the organization, to avoid waste in generating alternatives that may not be feasible for the library, to provide a motivating force, and to coordinate efforts and provide for consistent operations.

Overcoming the reluctance among staff to change is a critical first step in the strategy-formation process. The method used in conquering this natural inertia is extremely important. Setting goals that allow for participation in the decision-making process would be a good way to help the library staff accept the need for change and encourage acceptance and understanding of the strategy-formation activity.

Establishing goals has to be done on the basis of an imperfect knowledge of the future. Based on existing knowledge and predictions of the future, library managers have to make certain assumptions of what the future will bring in order to have coordinated, well-defined efforts in setting goals.

ASSUMPTIONS

Hussey defines an assumption as:

A statement of opinion about the occurrence of an event which is outside the control of the planner. This statement is treated as fact during the development of plans, although the judgment element must never be overlooked.[4]

Assumptions are factors that the planning team can state with almost complete certainty. For example, ''automation will play a prominent role in libraries in the 1980s'' is an assumption. The planning team will quickly recognize that there are many factors in the library's future that are unpredictable. The uncertainty of the future reinforces the need for developing strategies based on a logical structure. Assumptions serve to assist in the assessment of some of the risks the library faces and, in many instances, they can lead to actions that will reduce the risks.

Strategic planning cannot occur without assumptions. However, the assumptions must go beyond those that deal only with the continuation of current events. Assumptions are not to be based on mere guesswork. The environmental factors affecting libraries have to be carefully considered. Conclusions have to be drawn from relevant data, surveys, and trends. On occasion, planning assumptions may be perceived as opinion only. However, if the proper homework is done, the opinion is more likely than not to be correct.

GROUP SESSIONS

The evolvement of effective strategies is contingent upon the work of committees and task forces. These groups (members of the planning team) help to identify issues of concern and to generate new initiatives. They are important during the review of current goals and activities, in recognizing and giving priority to future goals, and in determining the paths for attaining goals and objectives. The group sessions bring forth new ideas and a screening process to evaluate the ideas. They provide a splendid forum for exercising creativity. Identification of targets of opportunities will be a useful by-product of brainstorming. Finding new opportunities for library service is a rewarding venture for the participants. Disciplined thinking will allow assessment of current and future opportunities, problems, and threats. To sustain a positive attitude during the ''give and take'' sessions, it is recommended that the groups operate from the existing strengths of the library.

When projecting the three- to five-year future of the library, the "multiple futures" approach should be used. For example, a future reflecting what the library "would like to be" should be projected. Another future might focus on what the library "is likely to be." And a third future could concentrate on the "extreme contrast" to the most probable case. Valuable insight into what would happen if the library followed one strategic goal and the exact opposite actually occurred is the greatest benefit to be gained by constructing an "extreme contrast" future. It is important to project a wide variety of alternative futures. Almost identical alternative futures lead to almost identical strategies, thus, defeating the exercise.

Written reports from the group sessions are encouraged. Each group should have a leader and a recorder. The participants should be informed that they can be freewheeling in their descriptions of the future. Also, each participant must take time to write what s/he desires the future of the library to be and what alternative courses of action must be taken to attain that future. The "backward analysis" approach should be used, that is, the participants should identify where the library should be in five years, then work back in time from the desired future to the present status of the library. During this regression, it is very important to identify how the library is to achieve desired future outcomes at which particular time in the five-year period. What pathways (i.e., strategies) should be pursued to attain the end results? Clarity and concrete statements should be basic elements of this written exercise. Do not worry about writing beautiful sentences. The main point is to record substantive thoughts in brief, understandable statements which can be analyzed, synthesized, and used in subsequent meetings.

Group interaction does not mean that strategy formulation and decision-making activities are turned over completely to subordinates; to follow this line of thinking might cause the library's effectiveness to deteriorate. Group interaction does refer to the process that transforms an aggregate of individuals into a cohesively functioning team or group. Time should be allotted for both individual and group problem-solving efforts. Some individuals are inhibited in group situations; furthermore, group participants sometimes tend to develop similar perceptions after working together. Thus, creativity, which is a very important part of strategy making, may be reduced unless independent individual problem solving activity is allowed. Individual creativity or problem solving may be enhanced if it follows a group-problem solving effort. Recognition and support should be given to individual problem-solving endeavors.

The planning team must set aside at least one day for its initial group session. Members must get away from their offices and "retreat" from any potential disturbances (e.g., telephone calls). The first meeting will likely be followed by smaller group meetings and, eventually, another full-group meeting. Also, department heads will need to meet with their respective departments to discuss strategy-formulation matters. All of these group sessions are crucial "keystones" for strategy formulation.

CHARACTERISTICS OF EFFECTIVE STRATEGY

There are various ways of assessing the effectiveness of a particular strategy. However, the first question one must address is whether or not the strategy matches the library's basic purposes. Is the strategy compatible with the library's environmental opportunities and resources? Also, there is the more subtle question of whether or not the strategy has been constructed in such a way that it facilitates the management processes of the organization.

While preparing strategy statements, great care needs to be taken to ensure that they are well-constructed. Hofer and Schendel have identified the following four characteristics of effective strategy statements:

1. The statements should describe each of the major components of the organization's strategy (e.g., its scope, resource deployments).
2. The statements should indicate how the strategy will lead to the accomplishment of the organization's goals and objectives.
3. The statements should be described in functional terms.
4. The statements should be as precise as possible.[5]

Explicitness must be one of the chief attributes of a strategy statement. After the strategy is made explicit, some basis exists for evaluating or improving it. But if strategy remains intuitive and no effort is made to explain and clarify its features, there will be ample room for the strategy to be misunderstood or be at cross-purposes with some (or many) of the organization's activities. The larger the library, the more urgent the need for explicit strategy. An explicit strategy will provide the library manager with a more sharply focused understanding of the library's role and the contribution s/he is expected to make to the determined goals and objectives. Explicit strategy statements should be perceived as ways for improving the overall performance of the library. The effectiveness of strategies can usually be gauged by the following six criteria:

1. *Internal consistency*. The strategy has to reflect consistency with the library's goals, objectives, and policies. New strategies must conform with the construct of existing strategies. All strategies for the library have to fit into an integrated pattern. The management structure has to accommodate all strategies and, therefore, there should be little or no conflict among them.

2. *Consistency with the external environment*. Strategies have to be in tune with the environment outside of the library. If a particular strategy runs counter to the intention of the publishing world, for example, then the library may have a very difficult time in collection development. The strategies used by a reference department must be geared to the needs of the library's users. Managers have to be conscious of the changing environment in which the library thrives. Strategies have to encompass the present situation as well as the future environment. Therefore, formulating a strategy is much like aiming at a moving target—one has to be concerned not only with the present position but also with the speed and direction of movement.

3. *Appropriateness in view of resources*. Does the library have the personnel, equipment, supplies, and operating budget necessary to implement and carry forth the strategy? This is an extremely important question to consider while determining the appropriateness of strategy. If a desired strategy requires a competence which is not held by anyone on the library's staff and if there are not any feasible alternatives for acquiring this particular talent, then it would be foolhardy for the library to pursue this strategy. Deployment of limited resources will have an impact on what strategies should be implemented. Some resources have to be categorized as "uncommitted" to allow positive action on unanticipated demands and opportunities.

4. *Acceptable degree of risk*. The resources of the library will chiefly determine the level of risk that can be taken. An effective strategy will not include a high-risk component if resources are not available or forthcoming. Long-term projects are normally more risky than short ones. Careful analysis is mandatory before the library can engage in a project involving high risk. Some libraries have gotten "burned" by computer vendors who could not deliver products within a specified time period. Episodes involving computer vendors going bankrupt or out of business are few in number.

Nevertheless, those libraries that have done business with these firms have, in some instances, been devastated as a result of the firms' discontinuance. One should not conclude from reading this that the best strategies have the least risk. The big payoffs frequently come with high-risk strategies. Just make sure to look before you leap.

5. *Appropriate timetable*. The time span for a strategy to be implemented and completed is a very significant part of strategy development. One has to be reasonable while setting the time horizon. The library's goals and objectives must be reviewed in detail prior to making a time-based strategy. Libraries, like ships, cannot be "spun on a dime." Strategies must be given sufficient time for complete implementation. The larger the library, the greater amount of time required for it to adjust to ramifications of strategies.

6. *Workability*. Does the strategy work? To meet the criteria of effectiveness, the chosen strategy has to work. Taylor and Hawkins conclude that two positive measures of a strategy's "workability" include the success in its execution and its favorable results.[6]

LEVELS OF STRATEGY

The library's complete strategy will consist of a hierarchical network of strategies made up of: (1) root strategy, (2) supporting functional area strategies, and (3) operating strategies.

The root strategy is the library's overall strategy. It is the umbrella strategy which is expressed in the library's mission statement. Also, it serves as the theme in the library's strategic plan and is the formulating basis for the supporting functional area strategies.

Supporting functional area strategies are designed to support the root strategy and to give overall direction to operating strategies. They are created in the upper echelons of library management (i.e., at the level of assistant director or above). A strategy to substantially reduce the backlog of uncataloged materials is an example of a supporting functional area strategy.

Operating strategies deal with the more specific departmental activities of the library, such as the head cataloger redirecting his/her staff from its regular activity to the task of processing a backlog of out-of-print materials. Tactics and operating strategies are often spoken of as being the same.

All of the strategies must be in harmony with one another and must be mutually reinforcing. They must be interlocking like the pieces of a puzzle. Without supporting functional strategies and operating strategies, the root statement will lack the completeness and operational specificity needed to give concrete guidance to the library and its departments. While each of the strategy elements has its own separate and distinct characteristic, they must be viewed as a whole and form a consistent strategic design. Thompson and Strickland emphasize that each successive level of strategy be logically derived from and consistent with the preceding level and, further, that there be a logical fit among the various strategic elements at each level.[7]

The following diagram reveals the hierarchical level and interdependence of the strategies:

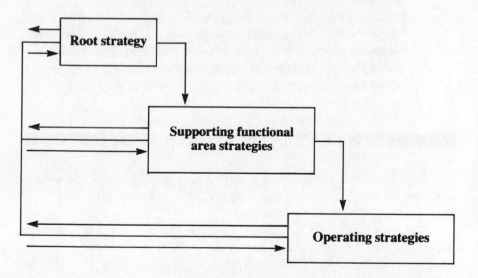

TYPES OF STRATEGIES

Due to the interrelatedness of strategies, it is difficult to separate them and create ones which are freestanding. Because the total library is a system with several subsystems (e.g., public services, technical services), it is a rare strategy that affects only one area of the library. Nevertheless, the major strategies which give the library an overall direction are likely to be in the following seven areas:

1. *Organizational strategies*. These strategies encompass the library's purpose and organizational design. They provide guidance for the library's administrative processes and policies. They answer questions such as how centralized decision-making authority should be, what departments are going to be merged to form a more efficient operation, and what the reporting structure should be. The organization structure will provide the system of roles and role relationships to help staff better accomplish the library's goals and objectives.
2. *Personnel strategies*. A wide variety of personnel strategies will have to be used to properly locate the right person for the right job assignment, to adequately reward the high performers, to ensure that affirmative action and equal opportunity practices are carried out, and to do the wide range of other duties and responsibilities so vital to this very important area of human resources.
3. *Growth strategies*. These strategies will deal with "where" and "when" growth is needed for specific areas of the library. Will the growth in one area (e.g., adding a new branch library) occur at the expense of another area (e.g., the central library)? How can growth be coordinated in order to have a favorable impact on the total library system?
4. *Opportunistic strategies*. Targets of opportunities appear on the horizon for all libraries at some propitious time. Preparation is the key in capitalizing on the opportunities. Managers sometimes must examine the areas of potential opportunities in a hasty fashion. Timing is of utmost importance while dealing with this type of strategy.
5. *Innovation strategies*. Something *new* and something *different* make up the main thrust of innovation strategies. Calculated risk is recommended during the introduction of new services and operations. If the product or process has not been validated in another library, the alpha library must proceed with caution while working with the innovation. An innovative strategy does not focus on the existing situation or practices. Rather, it is aimed at creating distinguishably new concepts of value and thereby generating a significant impact on the environment. According to Thompson and Strickland, creating novelty, altering appearance, or adding new variations to existing services does not qualify as innovation. They emphasize that innovation strategies are concerned with satisfying a want or performing a service in a manner that sets it apart from existing operations or services.[8]

6. *Financial strategies*. Every library manager has to be concerned with how his/her library is going to receive adequate funding. What courses of action will reap the most funds for the library? How can the library receive a higher priority by the funding agency? These are typical questions to be considered while formulating financial strategies.

7. *Retrenchment strategies*. Retrenchment has been common since the 1970s and it is expected to be with us throughout the 1980s. The national and world economy has taken its toll on the quality of library services. Many libraries have been ill-prepared when asked to reduce their budgets. Retrenchment strategies are commonly short-run endeavors to be used until the economy makes a recovery. It is incumbent on the library's planning team to design strategies that are long-range enough to cope with major financial reductions. In other words, a retrenchment strategy should not be perceived as a ''band-aid'' solution to the library's budgetary problems. Strategies must include the impact made on services in the affected area, the possibility of discontinuation of some services in lieu of reducing more vital services, and an anticipatory clause for dealing with the retrenchment issue on a multiyear basis.

SPECIFIC LIBRARY AREAS FOR STRATEGIC DEVELOPMENT

In addition to the seven overall general strategies, much work must be done on strategy formation for specific library areas. These areas include:

- Access services (e.g., circulation, current periodical service).
- Public services (e.g., reference, branch libraries, children's story hour).
- Technical services (e.g., cataloging, serial records).
- Collection development.
- Technology (e.g., online systems, bibliographic utilities).
- Resource sharing.
- Public relations.
- Special services (e.g., photocopying, preservation).
- Nonprint media.
- Physical facilities.

The types and number of specific areas for strategy development will depend upon the type of library. Department heads will play a very active role in developing the strategies in these areas.

INTERRELATIONSHIP OF STRATEGIES

Strategy is the conceptual glue that holds together the diverse, complex areas of the library. The strategies used by a library are interconnected and dependent on one another. They are not developed in isolation and cannot function apart from the rest of the library. Vancil explains the linking and compatibility of strategies this way:

> To be effective, strategy must personally affect each manager, containing the scope of his activities to some extent yet providing him with enough elbow room to devise his own strategy within the broader context. In such organizations it is not very useful to think about *the* strategy. Rather, one should think of the strategy as a collection of strategies, one for each manager, linked together by a progressive series of agreements on objectives, constraints and policies, and plans and goals. Each manager must have a strategy in which he believes and is compatible with the strategies of his superiors, his peers, and his subordinates.[9]

The term "department head" could be substituted for "manager" in applying Vancil's thoughts to a dynamic library setting.

Strategies, over a period of time, will emerge in a pattern of substrategies and intrastrategies. Consequently, the planning team will likely cluster similar strategies. The clustering of strategies will enhance the library's attempt to systematically achieve planned change in its service and operational programs.

SYNERGY

The interdependence of strategies and library programs should be used as an advantage during the formulation of strategy. Using the benefits of combined efforts is one positive feature of strategy development.

When two actions performed jointly produce a larger result than they would if performed independently, synergy exists. Synergy is an example of $2+2=5$. It is an important element in strategy development; however, it will not just happen, it must be planned for and made to happen.

ECONOMIES OF SCALE

A library realizes economies of scale when the total fixed costs of productive capacity are allocated among a larger number of products or services. Like synergy, economies of scale must be made to happen.

Two excellent examples of economies of scale are: (1) the introduction of wide-bodied jets by the airlines, enabling them to fly twice as many passengers with the same number of high-salaried pilots and flight engineers, and (2) the multiple-unit motion picture theatre that uses just one refreshment stand and ticket booth, thus requiring less floor space and fewer people to operate them.[10]

TRADEOFFS

Being able to identify when it is wise to trade off high targets of opportunities for low targets or vice versa, the strategist can successfully select and develop the action plan necessary to attain the established goals and objectives of the library. Trading off one opportunity for another to achieve the desired strategy requires a rational approach by the library manager. However, one's personal assessment of which choices are the best for the library will, undoubtedly, contain some unabashed subjectivity.

The library strategist seeks to reconcile conflicting forces during strategy formulation. S/he must deal simultaneously with four questions: (1) What *might* we do? (2) What *can* we do? (3) What do we *want* to do? and (4) What *should* we do?

STRATEGIC GAP

The strategic gap is the shortcoming the library will have between its optimum goal and its improvement target over a specified time period. ''Gap analysis'' is performed when the library examines what is entailed to move from the improvement target to the optimum goal. Filling this gap is what strategy is all about. This gap will only be filled if the library enters into new strategies.

The following diagram depicts the strategic gap:

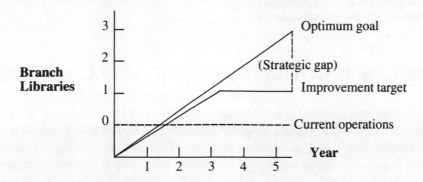

Optimum goal: To build three branch libraries in five years.

According to this strategic gap chart, if one branch (public) library is constructed within the first three years, an "improvement target" beyond the existing situation has been achieved. The next step for the planning team is that of carefully analyzing what effective strategies have to be deployed to achieve the optimum goal involving the construction of two additional branch libraries within the next two years.

In order to get the two additional branch libraries, some strategies may include: (1) beginning a massive "support for the library" campaign involving the local residents, (2) presenting a well-organized, informative program to the city council and mayor (e.g., depicting new services offered, space problems at the main library) on the benefits to be realized by the new branch libraries, (3) presenting facts on the demographics of the area(s) (e.g., number of persons without convenient library service) to the news media, and (4) utilizing the efforts and political influence of the library's board of trustees. One must never forget that the construction, staffing, development of the collection, and general operating expenses of a branch library cannot be funded at the expense of the main library. New money from passage of a bond or reallocation of funds from another city agency are the two best ways to construct branch libraries. The library director has to accept the fact that s/he will need to be armed with the best strategies possible while competing with other city agencies for budget increases.

Filling the strategic gap will require careful analysis of the available options and vigorous action on the part of the planning team—especially the library director. Analysis is very important; however, too much time should not be spent on reading tea leaves and trying to second-guess what the future may bring. The library's movers and shakers must think strategically and mount courses of action that will bring forth the funding necessary for the branch libraries. Creating and implementing these strategies is an exciting feature of strategic planning.

■ LINKING STRATEGY WITH OPERATIONS ■

Strategies should not be formed without some consideration of the short-term operating plans; however, strategy sets direction and must come before the day-to-day actions in the library. Library managers must realize that failure to separate strategy formulation from operations compromises the essence of strategic planning. Greater detail is found as one moves from strategy down to the operational level.

Regardless of the clear distinction between strategy and operations, library planners have to be aware of the relationship between the two. A winning combination for the strategy-formulation process is to have clear, understandable strategy followed by effective operations. If the strategy is understandable but the operations are ill-planned, the result will be uncertain. Actions and decisions at the lowest level in the library must occur within the context of the strategic framework.

■ EVALUATION ■

During the creation of strategies, the planning team needs to agree on basic evaluation criteria and techniques to use while assessing strategies. Consistency should prevail as much as possible during the evaluation process. Since strategies are, in a sense, hypotheses to be tested, it is difficult to have one evaluation technique for appraising all strategies. Each strategy problem and its solution is unique, thus compounding the evaluation process. Political and other real-world factors add to the complexity of strategy assessment.

Palmour et al. noted the criteria against which strategies should be evaluated:

1. Contribution to the library's goals and objectives.
2. Costs in staff time and other resources, and the effect on other services or programs of possible diversion of resources to the new activity.[11]

The most practical way of evaluating strategies is to ask the right question at the proper time. Each planning team has to compile its own unique list of questions. Following are samples of some random questions that might be asked when assessing library strategies:

1. Is the strategy realistic?
2. Is the strategy too risky?
3. Does the strategy conform with your library's goals and objectives?
4. Is the strategy clear and understandable by all appropriate library personnel?
5. Is the strategy acceptable?
6. Is the strategy legal?
7. Is the strategy in conformance with the library's internal and external environments?
8. Does the strategy under consideration conflict with other strategies being used by the library?
9. Does the strategy leave the library vulnerable to external competing forces?
10. Does the strategy capitalize on the library's strengths?
11. Does the strategy avoid the library's primary weaknesses?
12. Is there a possible conflict between the proposed strategy and existing policy?
13. Is the strategy consistent with the philosophy of the library's parent organization?
14. Is the library's administrative structure capable of implementing the strategy?
15. Does the library have financial capability to implement and complete the strategy?
16. Will other areas of the library suffer if the strategy is funded?
17. Is the timing of the strategy appropriate?
18. Have all possible alternatives for the strategy been examined?
19. Is there a total library commitment to implement the strategy?
20. Are there adequate physical facilities to accommodate the strategy?
21. Is there a refinement process for the strategy?
22. Will the strategy cause any drastic deviation from vital library services?
23. Have the users been kept in mind while developing the strategies?

24. Is the strategy capable of being implemented in an efficient and effective manner?
25. Has the strategy been tested or implemented in other library settings?

REFERENCES

1. John G. Hutchinson, *Management Strategy and Tactics* (New York: Holt, Rinehart and Winston, 1971), p. 49.

2. Charles W. Hofer and Dan Schendel, *Strategy Formulation: Analytical Concepts* (St. Paul, MN: West Publishing Company, 1978), p. 44.

3. Frank T. Paine and William Naumes, *Organizational Strategy and Policy: Text Cases and Incidents* (Philadelphia, PA: W. B. Saunders Co., 1975), p. 277.

4. David E. Hussey, *Introducing Corporate Planning,* 2nd Edition (New York: Pergamon Press, 1979), p. 62.

5. Hofer and Schendel, p. 42.

6. Bernard Taylor and Kevin Hawkins, *A Handbook of Strategic Planning* (London: Longman, 1972), pp. 53–63.

7. Arthur A. Thompson and A. J. Strickland, *Strategy and Policy: Concepts and Cases* (Dallas, TX: Business Publications, Inc., 1978), pp. 45–46.

8. Thompson and Strickland, pp. 79–80.

9. Richard F. Vancil, "Strategy Formulation in Complex Organizations," in *Strategic Planning Systems,* ed. Peter Lorange and Richard F. Vancil (Englewood Cliffs, NJ: Prentice-Hall, Inc. 1977), p. 21.

10. Dan R. E. Thomas, "Strategy Is Different In Service Businesses," *Harvard Business Review* 56 (July–August 1978): 160.

11. Vernon E. Palmour et al., *A Planning Process for Public Libraries* (Chicago: American Library Association, 1980), p. 70.

5

ALTERNATIVES AND CONTINGENCIES

66 The thing to do with the future is not to forecast it, but to create it. The objective of planning should be to design a desirable future and to invent ways to bring it about. 99

—*Russell Ackoff*

Libraries have to cope with several political, economical, and technological changes and uncertainties, requiring the best of one's creativity. To accomplish the library's goals and objectives, it may be necessary to use a creative approach. The strategist asks: Given the resources at the library's disposal, what strategic alternatives are available? Is there an opportunity for uncommon, innovative strategies? Can strategies be clustered in order to achieve goals and objectives? If our strategy does not unfold as anticipated, what contingency action plan will be used? When things go awry, what contingencies will ''save'' the affected library program?

ALTERNATIVES

The discovery of strategic alternatives is not a passive activity. Library managers cannot wait for things to happen; they are responsible for making things happen. Thus, it is important to keep an open mind while determining how the strategic net should be cast when fishing for alternatives. Brainstorming, idea sessions, and independent thought are ways to seek alternative approaches to opportunities and to suppress or overcome weaknesses and threats. Ideas for alternative courses of action should also be encouraged from persons outside of the library's formal structure. For example, patrons may furnish valuable ideas if they are permitted the chance to express their opinions of how services should be improved.

The library planning team enhances its effectiveness by working in small groups. Each group could create a list of alternate strategies for attaining a particular goal or objective. Paine and Naumes explain the dynamics of the group activity:

> The group activity should be structured so that the relevant people are there. The relevant people are those most directly affected by the opportunity or problem and those with necessary skills and knowledge. The consequences may involve intact work teams or ad hoc work groups. There may be separate action planning by teams at all levels. Preplanning of the group composition is, of course, an important feature in structuring the activity. The group sessions should be structured to open lines of communication and, through the use of group dynamics, to establish personal and group commitment to improving strategy development and implementation. The aim is to identify major strategy issues and opportunities, to identify barriers to organization effectiveness, to establish a readiness to act, and to develop a plan of specific action for relevant parties.[1]

Department heads should involve various members of the units in the development of alternatives for accomplishing the agreed-upon objective(s). Alternatives developed at the departmental level provide an example of a shared approach to problem solving. Moreover, this type of activity (1) produces positive changes in line and staff attitudes regarding strategic planning and (2) creates a means for improving effectiveness in the department's problem-solving and cooperative abilities.

Continuing with Existing Strategy

If a particular strategy is working effectively, is there reason to abandon it? Naturally, it is tempting to stay with a proven strategy in lieu of pursuing an untested, unknown alternative path. This temptation is all the more reason for the strategist to pose some searching questions in conducting an evaluation of this alternative. Thompson and Strickland offer the following questions:

1. Precisely what does the current strategy have going for it?
2. Why is it better than other alternatives?
3. Is re-affirmation of the status quo strategy the result of a hard-nosed review or laziness?
4. Is it justified on the basis of risk preference or is it just convenient?
5. Is "more of the same" predicated on a timely "wait and see" attitude or on a desire to escape the unpleasantries of change?[2]

If it is decided that the life cycle of the current strategy has not yet been completed, one needs to make provision for "fine-tuning" the strategy. Every successful strategy sows seeds of its own obsolescence through the new realities and problems it creates; therefore, modifications are mandatory in any ongoing strategy. A strategy is seldom static, but it is evolving until it fulfills its life expectancy.

Recovery

As a consequence of financial woes in recent years, several libraries have made drastic cuts in services and collections. In many incidents, alternative strategies were considered while libraries were absorbing the reductions in budget or eliminating services. If funds are restored or if funds are redirected back to those areas where reductions/eliminations were made, then recovery strategies will be necessary. Alternative recovery strategies require top-priority treatment by library management. Successful strategies from previous years may be recycled or reformulated.

Short-Range versus Long-Range Alternatives

The strategy-formation process requires both short- and long-range alternatives. Short-range alternatives deal with strategies that have a life cycle of one year or less while long-range alternatives last for two to five years.

Too often, managers think exclusively in terms of short-range planning, since it is easy to project and attain immediate results. However, the small problems of today might be replaced by the major crises of tomorrow if one exercises only the short-range mentality. For example, a short-range alternative for meeting the immediate demands in circulation procedures might be to purchase a turnkey circulation control system. But, in the long run, it may be better to slowly develop an effective total (online) library system (i.e., circulation, public access catalog, acquisitions, serials control) over a five-year period.

Regardless of the urgency to consider long-range benefits in lieu of short-term conveniences, it is noteworthy to understand that some alternative strategies have to be short-range. Limited financial resources can dictate whether or not a program has to be implemented/completed in one year or less.

Narrowing the Choice

After a list of viable strategic alternatives has been developed for each goal/objective, it is time to begin the process of narrowing the list of alternatives. The strategic planning team has to identify which alternatives enhance the current strengths of the library. Building on existing attributes is of prime importance. Libraries serve, in essence, as "all things to all people." However, new programs will have to be built on prevailing pockets of excellence. During the process of eliminating alternatives, it is noteworthy to match desired alternatives with existing competence on the library staff. If the alternative selected is expected to come to fruition as a result of existing library staff performance, then the qualifications of the staff become paramount. Further, those alternatives that do not comply with the library's mission should not be given serious consideration.

Flexibility is another desired characteristic of alternatives. Can the alternative be implemented, in part this year, then in full during ensuing years? How flexible will the alternative be in an unpredicted circumstance? If the alternative is so rigid that it cannot be modified to meet the library's needs, then it should be dropped.

Alternatives that obviously are contrary to basic functions of libraries should be eliminated. For example, a measure promoting censorship should not even be considered. Obvious library weaknesses that cannot be overcome or areas that should not be developed (e.g., building a collection on the Pre-Raphaelite period in a small, rural library when there is nominal interest in the topic) should receive little or no attention.

In narrowing the list of alternatives, one may want to place some of the "discarded" alternatives in a reserve capacity for future consideration. The changing external environment may impose a threat or opportunity that may make a reserve alternative more viable.

The chosen alternatives must permit the opportunity to deviate, if necessary, from the planned strategy. Hussey believes that a rigid plan which demands a blind allegiance is not a good plan, and a rigid management is not a good management.[3] With this flexibility in mind, the strategist's task becomes one of reconciling the pros and cons of the remaining alternatives. Trade-offs must be used to gain the optimum benefits from the alternative paths. Compromises must be made to exploit every opportunity to its fullest. One must be careful, for maximizing the library's strengths could mean concomitant increases in the chances of failure in other areas of library programs. The best thing to do is find the alternative offering the most satisfactory blend of advantages and disadvantages. The leading alternatives should be examined from the following angles:

1. Which strategic alternative offers the best match with the library's financial resources?
2. Which alternative promises to make the greatest contribution to overall library performance?
3. Which alternative offers the most dominant competitive edge to forces in the library's external environment? How vulnerable is this candidate to possible strategic forces in the external environment?
4. Which alternative minimizes the creation of new (and perhaps thorny) operating or administrative problems?
5. Which alternative has the best combination of high expected service improvement and low-risk exposure?
6. Which alternative offers the most favorable trade-off between maximizing opportunities and minimizing weaknesses?
7. Which alternative appears best suited to the library's management know-how, philosophy, personality, and sense of social responsibilities?
8. Which of the leading alternatives appear most propitious from the standpoint of timing? Is now the opportune time to be bold or cautious, a leader or a follower? Which strategy offers the best trade-off among near-term, long-term, and flexibility goals/objectives?
9. Which alternative, if successful, would provide the best platform for taking advantage of other opportunities that might present themselves?[4]

One may want to quantify the process of selecting the "best" alternative by assigning "weights" to each alternative. But one cannot deduct the best alternative based on a simple plus and minus rating system, because some factors should be given more weight than others, depending upon the particular library's overall strategy.

During the final deductions, many decisions will be based on judgment. Facts and analysis will be of tremendous value during the decision-making process, but they will not resolve conflicts and inconsistencies. The library director will have to "bite the bullet" in making hard choices which will be in the best interest of the library as a whole. Intuition, personal experiences, institutional good, qualitative trade-offs, value preferences, intangible situational factors, and compromise of opinion become an integral part of the process of making a strategic commitment. And no formula or how-to-do-it description is ever likely to take their place. In the final planning process, planners will actually not choose one total plan of action from among the alternatives proposed but instead pick and choose from several sets of proposals. In this manner, the organizational strategy chosen is not only consistent and feasible but also acceptable to more individuals within the library. Setting alternatives also allows library management some contingency in the event that one of the plans of action is unacceptable for some unanticipated reason.

CONTINGENCIES

Strategic planning is based on activities and events that have a high probability of occurring—the most likely happenings. However, there are less likely conditions that could cause serious problems for a library if they actually occurred. These uncertain conditions create the need for contingency planning. Contingency planning is making preparations to take specific actions when an event or condition not planned for in the formal planning process actually does take place. Since there is one constant—the future is unpredictable—it is advisable to develop "contingencies," regardless of how good the strategic plan is. Steiner describes the fundamental purpose of contingency planning as follows:

> To place managers in a better position to deal with unexpected developments than if they had not made such preparations. By failing to anticipate certain events, managers may not act as quickly as they should in a critical situation and the event may create more damage than it otherwise would have. Contingency planning should eliminate fumbling, uncertainty, and time delays in making the needed response to an emergency. Contingency planning also should make such responses more rational.[5]

Contingencies are used in libraries in response to an imminent and intensifying threat to existing activities. The incorporation of contingencies into the strategic planning process has several advantages, most of which relate to the ease with which the transition from one strategy alternative to another can be made once an event that has been foreseen as possible actually occurs. Radford believes the absence of crisis and of the disruption that it sometimes produces is often realized as the most important and productive of these advantages.[6]

Contingency planning is an integral part of identifying and selecting alternative strategies. After a careful investigation of contingencies, the library's strategies and alternative strategies may be modified to generate a more flexible stance. Hussey describes those strategic courses of action reserved for contingency purposes in this way:

> One point that is overlooked in the preparation of strategic plans is that the information available at the time the plan is made will vary in quality between strategies, and between one plan and the next. It is therefore not possible for the organization to write down each of its strategies with the same degree of exactitude. Some strategic paths will be crude lines on the organization's map of its future; others will be painted in finite detail and every bump in the road identified and understood. To attempt to delay the plan until all strategies can be identified with equal confidence would mean that no plan was ever produced. The problem is that any plan is but a strategic photograph of a dynamic scene. It is pleasant to visualize a situation where plans are all neat and tidy, when things can be labeled and pigeonholed, and where the strategic plan can, accordingly, be used as a handbook for a sequence of actions the effect of which is known to the last halfpenny. But we live in a real world, not a fairyland, and it is only occasionally that an organization will find its strategic plan fits so neatly into place that there is nothing to do over the next five to ten years, but sit back and watch it all happen. The real world is untidy: so most strategic plans will contain some loose areas with ragged edges.[7]

If the planning team is developing contingencies for the first time, it should keep the process as simple as possible. Contingencies tend to be downside and people do not like to anticipate negative situations. If people do not like to plan in general, contingency planning becomes an even more difficult task.

Following are some guidelines recommended by Linneman that should be kept in mind when developing contingency actions:

1. Keep the plans simple. Avoiding complex plans will make preparation easier.

2. Consider positive as well as negative reactions. Positive actions help to improve morale. Furthermore, they are more likely to improve productivity.
3. Estimate the funding necessary for implementing the contingency action. Make sure funding requirements are realistic and available.[8]

REFERENCES

1. Frank T. Paine and Willam Naumes, *Organizational Strategy and Policy: Text Cases and Incidents* (Philadelphia, PA: W. B. Saunders Company, 1975), p. 246

2. Arthur A. Thompson and A. J. Strickland, *Strategy and Policy: Cases and Concepts* (Dallas, TX: Business Publications, Inc., 1978), p. 88.

3. David E. Hussey, *Introducing Corporate Planning,* 2nd Edition (New York: Pergamon Press, 1979), p. 80.

4. Thompson and Strickland, pp. 103–04.

5. George A. Steiner, *Strategic Planning: What Every Manager Must Know* (New York: Free Press, 1979), pp. 229–30.

6. K. J. Radford, *Strategic Planning: An Analytical Approach* (Reston, VA: Reston Publishing Co., 1980), p. 149.

7. David E. Hussey, *Corporate Planning: Theory and Practice,* 2nd Edition (New York: Pergamon Press, 1982), pp. 180–81.

8. Robert E. Linneman, *Shirt-Sleeve Approach to Long-Range Planning for the Smaller, Growing Corporations* (Englewood Cliffs, NJ: Prentice-Hall, 1980), pp. 211–12.

6

POLICIES

66 If we could first know where we are tending, we could then better judge what to do and how to do it. **99**

—Abraham Lincoln

Policy concerns the library's methods, procedures, and practices associated with implementing and executing strategy. Policies give direction to how the library will be managed and are the understandings (written, oral, or implicit) designed to set perimeters to the thinking and action of the library staff.

Strategy tells us how the library's mission, goals, and objectives are to be achieved, while policy guides and controls strategy implementation. Policy is essentially a framework with specific guidelines under which operations of the library fall. It is subordinate to and supportive of the mission, goals, objectives, and strategy.

The following illustration depicts the relationships among the library's mission, goals, objectives, strategy, and policy:

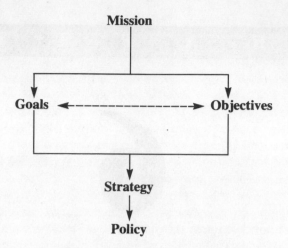

Policies, as guidelines to action, are usually based on past experiences. The strategic planners take a comprehensive view of the library's mission, goals, objectives, and strategy; the policymaker operates in a more limited vein. Policy is basically an ongoing procedure to help management solve specific problems, such as preventing errors from recurring, and implement and test strategy. According to Reinharth, there is obviously a means-end relationship among the mission, goals, objectives, strategy, and policies.[1] The means-end relationship occurs because the mission, goals, objectives, strategies, and policies are all linked to one another.

STATING POLICIES

A policy has to be more than a platitude. It should be a helpful guide to making strategy explicit. Therefore, the more definite the policy is, the more helpful it will be for the library staff, patrons, and others who may want to peruse it. To ensure the maximum possible clarity and to prevent inconsistent interpretations, policies should be in written form. If they are to serve as "road maps" which chart the day-to-day operations of the library, then the library staff is entitled to see them in writing. Policies are mandatory for a library if it purports to be well-managed. The managerial functions of policy are summarized by Thompson and Strickland:

1. Policy promotes *uniform handling* of similar activities. It creates a uniformity which facilitates better coordination of work tasks and helps reduce friction arising from favoritism, discrimination, and disparate handling of common functions.

2. Policy introduces *continuity of action and decisions* throughout the library. It minimizes zig-zag behavior and conflicting actions and establishes some degree of order, regularity, stability, and dependability in both the library's internal and external relationships.
3. Policy acts as an *automatic decision maker* by formalizing library-wide answers to previously made management decisions about how particular questions and problems should be resolved. It becomes a guide for handling future such problems or issues as they recur without their being passed up through higher management echelons again and again.
4. Policy offers a *predetermined answer to routine problems* and gives key decision makers more time to cope with nonroutine matters. Through this method, decisions pertaining to both ordinary and extraordinary problems are greatly expedited; the former by referring to established policy and the latter by drawing upon a portion of the decision maker's current time.
5. Existing policies afford managers *a mechanism for insulating* themselves from hasty and ill-considered requests for a policy change. The prevailing policy can always be used as a reason (or excuse) for not yielding to expedient or temporarily valid arguments for policy revisions.
6. Policy serves a *major communication link* to the library's several constituents. External policy statements aid patrons in appraising library behavior and performance. Internal policy statements not only illustrate to library staff what sort of actions and decisions are appropriate, but they also assist in casting the library's character and personality.[2]

Ideally, policies flow from the library's strategy; they can relate either to administrative matters or to operating procedures. The managerial thrust of policy is to set organizational mechanisms in place that will support strategic success.

The larger the library, the greater the need to have policies stated in writing, but each library must decide how codified a system it requires. To be effective, a policy must be narrow enough to govern managerial activity without obstructing individual initiative and creativity. Nor should it require continual adjustment; its purpose is to ensure stability, not undercut it. Of course, times do change, and policies must be accommodated to fit them.

POLICY FORMULATION

A crucial determinant of the library's effectiveness is communicating the mission, goals, objectives, and strategies to persons within the library structure and external constituents. This is usually done through the formulation of policies. Without such policies, the library managers have no framework for effective decision making.

How should library policy be formulated? What should the policy formulation process include? The director's office must not make policy in isolation. Policy making, if it is to be effective, has to involve staff throughout the library. Also, governing boards, committees, library trustees, and other appropriate advisory groups will play a major part in some of the more far-reaching policies. When department heads and supervisors realize that their experience and judgment are valued and their input is accepted (not just asked for and then ignored), the policy formulation process will be more effective. Whittaker notes "that this stands to reason, for the end result is not, as some might argue, the formulation of the policy."[3] The end result is that, after the policy has been formulated, library employees will be able to act accordingly when they encounter a situation in which the new policy is applicable.

Policy is a sort of "decision rule" in the way that it signals what should and should not be done in order to further the achievement of strategy. The library's management structure dictates the need for both major and minor policies. The scope of library policy may range from such lofty principles as "It is our policy to provide full reference service to all persons" and "We are an equal opportunity employer" down to more mundane matters as "We circulate books for 14 days."

Some policies concern operating procedures and amount to little more than work rules, as in the case of statements specifying the length of coffee breaks and the methods for obtaining reimbursement for travel expenses. Other policies provide vital support to the library's strategic plan. Some examples are:

1. It is our policy to develop a book collection devoid of any censorship practices.
2. We are going to implement an online acquisitions subsystem prior to a serials control subsystem.
3. Our policy is to expand the central library in lieu of building branch libraries.

TYPES OF POLICIES

There are many types of policies that affect libraries. Evans has identified four types of policies that are common to libraries:

1. *Originated policy*. The strategic planning team would generate major, basic policies and then disseminate these policies throughout the library. General and minor policies are formulated at the departmental level. The general and minor policies are made with the understanding that they match or support the originated policies.

2. *Appealed policy*. This type of policy results from a circumstance for which there is no policy. Someone in the lower echelon of the library cannot determine what to do in a particular situation and, as a consequence of not having access to a policy on the matter, starts the identified problem up the chain of command. The problem is invariably passed up the pecking order in an attempt to get an answer. The appealed policies consume valuable time; however, they appear to be unavoidable, regardless of how much forethought and preparation are given to the library's policy-formulation process.

3. *Implied policy*. This policy evolves when people believe what they see or hear as policy. In other words, people conclude that the real policy is what is being done, not what is contained in the stated policy. A dichotomous situation exists with the administration following the stated policy while staff at the operational level are functioning under the implied policy. Such a circumstance can be dangerous and demoralizing. It is incumbent upon the library administration to make the stated policy available to all parties concerned. Implied policies must be held to a minimum.

4. *Externally imposed policy*. There have always been some non-library imposed policies. Certain laws, for example, have restricted what libraries can or cannot do. State and federal government have, for some time, issued guidelines for certain libraries (e.g., public, school, and state library agencies).[4]

In recent years, more externally imposed policies have affected libraries. Unions, for example, have brought forth their employee-relations policies (e.g., promotion criteria). Individuals who donate valuable book collections are likely to request specific restrictions. It is anticipated that the externally imposed policies will increase, rather than lessen, in number.

Regardless of the various types of policies, it must be remembered that they are all to be treated in the context of their means-end relationship with strategy. Policies are to provide the guidelines used by library managers while they are instigating and implementing strategy.

REFERENCES

1. Leon Reinharth et al., *The Practice of Planning: Strategic, Administrative, and Operational* (New York: Van Nostrand Reinhold, 1981), pp. 33–34.
2. Arthur A. Thompson and A. J. Strickland, *Strategy and Policy: Concepts and Cases* (Dallas, TX: Business Publications, Inc., 1978), pp. 22–23.
3. James B. Whittaker, *Strategic Planning in Rapidly Changing Environment* (Lexington, MA: Lexington Books, 1978), p. 48.
4. G. Edward Evans, *Management Techniques for Librarians* (New York: Academic Press, 1976), pp. 93–95.

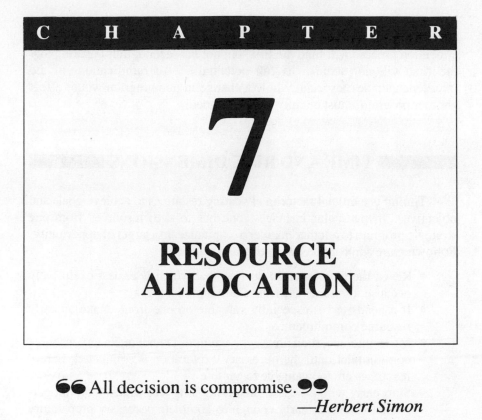

7

RESOURCE ALLOCATION

❝ All decision is compromise. ❞
—Herbert Simon

After the mission, goals, objectives, strategies, and policies have been placed in proper perspective by the planning team, the next area to receive attention is resource allocation. In this context, resources do not refer to financial resources only; they include personnel, physical facilities, time, and equipment. Both existing and new resources must be given consideration, although the focus here will be on strategic budgets, not operating budgets.

Strategy is implemented through the allocation of resources. One of the first steps in the allocation process is the ranking of priorities based on the library's goals and objectives. After the planning team has determined the priorities, department heads on the team should take the list to their respective departments for discussion. After this discussion has occurred, the planning team should reassemble to finalize the priority listing.

It is significant to consider the interdependencies of the programs and projects. King and Cleland claim that "a project's greatest value can only be achieved if a second project is also successful, and if the first project is rated more highly than the second, it is possible that a simple resource allocation process will fund the first, but not the second, thus ensuring that the first will not achieve its full potential."[1] All ramifications of the interdependencies, especially how a change in one program would affect another program, must be fully comprehended.

TIME AND RISK DIMENSIONS

Timing is a crucial factor in allocating resources to achieve goals and objectives. In particular instances, one has to shift resources from one strategic program to another in order to capitalize on a target of opportunity. Following are some guides on timing and sequence:

- Resist the temptation to do first that which is easiest exclusively because it requires the least amount of resources.
- If a head start is especially valuable on one front, make an early resource commitment.
- Move into uncertain areas with caution. Do not make any resource commitment until the necessary exploration is completed; library resources are too valuable to gamble.
- Start early with processes involving long lead times. Commit personnel resources early enough to complete necessary preparatory work. Murphy's Law states that "everything takes longer than anticipated."

King and Cleland note that the interrelationship of timing and risk is an important matter in strategic allocation decisions, as illustrated through questions such as: (1) Should we undertake this strategic project now or delay it until the situation becomes more clear (and less risky)? and (2) Would a commitment of resources now be warranted on the grounds that this activity will itself help resolve the uncertainty?[2]

Although timing delays may reduce uncertainty, they may result in lost opportunities. A balance in timing and risk-taking should be sought.

CRITICAL RESOURCES

Resources have to be related to the library's current and future conditions. They must be seen as dynamic—able to be reallocated among different library programs as conditions change—in order for the library to attain its goals and objectives. The library's strategic profile (e.g., its five-year plan) must be tied directly to all resource allocations.

Money

Money is more often than not an important strategic variable. Compounding the library's lack of money, many governing boards require that all funds be expended in a given fiscal year. This inability to carry funds over into the next year does not permit the latitude necessary for effective planning. Nearly every library has limits—some of them severe—on its resources. The tricky issue is how to use limited funds and time constraints in the most advantageous way.

Using available funds to support strategic programs and enlarging the budget through strategic efforts are two important endeavors for which the planning team needs to devote considerable time. The scarce resources phenomenon will undoubtedly demand much thinking and improvising.

Money is a particularly valuable resource because it provides the library with the greatest flexibility of response to events as they arise. It may be considered the "safest" resource in that safety may be equated with the freedom to choose from among the widest variety of future alternatives.

Competent Personnel

The personnel of the library are its most valuable resource. While determining strategy, the library planning team must make an honest appraisal of its staff to pinpoint exactly where its strengths and weaknesses are. Such an assessment must be done in confidence, due to the many sensitivities involved with the issue. The degree of competence should not be expected to be uniform throughout the library. Needless to say, the best people have to be assigned to key areas of the strategic plan.

The management dimension of the library is also critical. The depth of a library's management resources constitutes its greatest strategic constraint. In many ways, and in contrast to the financial aspects, this dimension is the most difficult to assess. Even though the following poem applies more to the corporate than to the library world, it serves the purpose of underscoring the requirement of a strong management dimension:

Though your balance sheet is a model
of what balance sheets should be
Typed and ruled with great precision
in a type that all can see.
Though the grouping of the assets
is commendable and clear
And the details which are given
more than usually appear.
Though investments have been valued
at the sale of each day
And the auditor's certificate shows
everything O.K. . . . . .
One asset is omitted—and its
worth I want to know:
That asset is the value
of the people who run the show.

—Author unknown

In essence, the strategic planning process and its results will be no better than the competence of the library management. The management includes all those professionals associated with the director's office and the department heads. To reiterate, the best managers have to be assigned to the most crucial roles of the strategic planning process.

Physical Facilities

This is an area that is frequently misunderstood in strategic planning. Facilities have no intrinsic value for their own sake. Their value to the library is usually expressed in space to house the collections, seating/study space for patrons, and equipment to perform necessary tasks.

Physical facilities have significance primarily in relations to overall library strategy. How, when, where, and why physical facilities are allocated to various departments or locations in the library are directly tied to the library's strategic design. For example, installing public access terminals throughout the library will support the library's goal of providing patron access to the bibliographic records and allowing specific circulation procedures to be transacted.

ACHIEVING THE RIGHT BALANCE

One of the most challenging issues in strategic planning is that of achieving a balance between goals/objectives and available library resources. This endeavor requires reliable estimates of the total library resources necessary to achieve particular goals and objectives, the rate at which they will have to be committed, and the likelihood that they will be available. The most common errors are either to fail to make these estimates at all or to be excessively optimistic about them. Committing funds to currently perceived opportunities and reserving a portion of funds for unexpected necessary projects are integral components of resource allocation in strategic planning.

REFERENCES

1. William R. King and David I. Cleland, *Strategic Planning and Policy* (New York: Van Nostrand Reinhold, 1978), p. 212.
2. King and Cleland, p. 213.

C H A P T E R

8

AN MIS FOR STRATEGIC PLANNING

❝The purpose of an MIS is to provide, as efficiently, effectively, and economically as possible, what management needs to know.❞
—*Herman Limberg*

Information is a vital cornerstone in the strategic planning process. It provides the basis for effective decision making. Unlike the approach of collecting information on overall operations of the library, the planning management information system (MIS) focuses on information that supports the development and implementation of strategy. MIS provides library management with the timely and relevant information it requires to assess the library's internal and external environment, monitor progress, detect trends, evaluate alternatives, and make decisions for optimum results.

King and Cleland emphasize that "data" and "information" are not to be treated synonymously in strategic planning. The word "data" means "facts" or simply informational raw materials. "Data" refers to unevaluated available symbols, whereas "information" refers to data that have been evaluated for some particular application or use.[1] Thus, strategic information represents data that have been evaluated to be of specific and identifiable use in the library's strategic planning process. The primary distinction between the two terms is that, while "information" consists of "data," not all data produce specific and meaningful information.

PRACTICAL ASPECTS OF LIBRARY INFORMATION

Management must have a sure grasp of all information pertaining to the library and all of its interrelated parts. Background information on all of the library's operations is necessary prior to any pretense of planning. Such information has to be shared with all members of the planning team. Many library operations are task-oriented and, therefore, productivity can be measured in specific terms. For example, one can equate the number of books cataloged with the number of librarians in the cataloging department. Library directors have recently become more conscious than ever about their library's internal operations; they have found they cannot function from an ivory tower. Cross analyses of service data (e.g., number of directional questions answered at an information desk) can be done with cost data (e.g., cost per directional answer). Information on cost-benefit projects will have a direct bearing on rational decision making.

Information files on special competencies of the staff (e.g., foreign language fluency) should be maintained and used when an opportunity arises. Unique attributes of the staff deserve consideration while developing strategies. Who can do what when? There is a positive correlation between the development of library policy and the information available on the staff.

Annual progress reports from individual library departments contain a wealth of information that can be used in planning. These departmental annual reports should be shared with other departments throughout the library system.

Information on political forces is crucial to the library's MIS. For example, a state library agency should know which legislators are enemies of libraries. Such information is necessary for developing a state library's strategic plan. Directors of public libraries should have an information profile on each city council member. These "banks" of information will help managers to strategically avoid nonsupporters of libraries and to dedicate their energies garnering support from "friends" of libraries.

For its greatest effectiveness, information has to be carefully monitored. Better and more complete information on the library is difficult to oppose. It is the obligation of library management to analyze its own library situation and devise a tailored MIS.

OBJECTIVES OF AN MIS

Essentially, an effective MIS has the following objectives:

- To facilitate the decision-making process in the library by providing the managers with accurate, timely, and selective information that assists them in determining a specific course of action.
- To provide for the objective performance measurements and assessments of selected relevant areas of the library. The areas are to be determined during strategic planning.
- To provide pertinent information about the library's internal and external environments.
- To provide information on alternative strategies and contingency plans.

Library managers will require specific information during the various stages of the strategic planning process. The following stages must have answers (information) to many relevant concerns and questions, including the examples given.

A. Library self-analysis (What is our current situation?)
   1. What have been our mission, goals, objectives, and strategies?
   2. What are our existing and what will be our future mission, goals, objectives, and strategies?
   3. What financial, physical, and personnel resources do we have?
   4. What are our current programs of library services?

B. Goals and objectives (What do we want our future to be?)
   1. Where do we want the library to be in five years?
   2. What new service programs can we implement?
   3. How can we measure our progress toward goals and objectives?
   4. What opportunities can we pursue?

C. Identification of attributes (What are our major strengths?)
1. On which strengths do we build?
2. Which service programs should we combine in order to gain strength?
3. In which library departments do we have "superstars?" How can we use their talents more effectively?

D. Identification of constraints and weaknesses (What might inhibit us?)
1. What major weaknesses do we have?
2. What future circumstances will affect us?
3. What laws or externally imposed policies might affect us?
4. What external-environment competitive forces might affect our services?

E. Formulation of strategy (What means do we adopt?)
1. What results can be expected from our strategic alternatives?
2. What are the risks involved with each strategic course of action?
3. What can we do to guarantee that the strategies will be developed well enough to achieve our expected outcomes?
4. How will the strategies be evaluated?

F. Action plans (What implementation mechanism will be used?)
1. What courses of action are to be performed?
2. Who is going to do them?
3. What results will be sought?
4. When will each course of action be completed?
5. What resources will be required?
6. What guidelines and assumptions underlie the projected results?

The information brought forth by the preceding questions will help create the central core of the strategic-planning MIS. Information is required for two primary needs during the strategic planning activity: (1) the need for establishing a base for planning and (2) the need for having a means for controlling and monitoring performance.

MIS PLANNING STEPS

There are at least a dozen MIS planning steps to use with the library's strategic planning. They are:

1. *Define purpose*. During this step, the overall mission/purpose of the total MIS is made explicit. All persons on the planning team should participate in defining the purpose of the MIS.
2. *Define objectives*. This step goes hand-in-glove with defining the purpose of the MIS. Objectives and purposes of the MIS should closely parallel the mission, goals, and objectives of the library.
3. *Identify external forces*. Many external forces or systems exist that affect the library or are affected by it. For example, some of the forces are tax reductions, high inflation, uncertain public support, aggressive computer vendors, and changing state and federal laws.
4. *Outline internal forces*. This step is similar to step 3, except that the MIS addresses the forces within the library. Examples include: (1) increased use of collections, (2) impact of technology on competence of existing personnel, and (3) worn-out, ineffective equipment. In addition to the present forces, the positive and negative forces of the future should be identified.
5. *Identify present and future information subsystems*. In addition to identifying all present and future subsystems within the library, the subsystems' purposes, structures, content, and interrelationships are to be delineated with as much accuracy as possible.
6. *Identify present information subsystems working well*. These subsystems do not require any major change and may now be included in the total library MIS.
7. *Identify present information subsystems requiring modifications*. These subsystems require major changes prior to being incorporated into the library's MIS.
8. *Identify future information subsystems requiring implementation*. This step focuses on pinpointing these highly important future subsystems which must be included in the MIS.
9. *Consider development approaches*. At this juncture, the preliminary design of the total MIS is given consideration. Emphasis is on the various alternative approaches that are available in the development, the implementation of each information subsystem, and the integration of these subsystems into the total library MIS.
10. *Give priority to subsystems*. Before the priorities are assigned, each subsystem is subjected to a thorough analysis. The analysis includes: (a) description of the direct and indirect burdens and benefits of each subsystem; (b) evaluation of the merits of each subsystem; (c) estimation of the resources required for the de-

velopment, conversion, and operation of each subsystem; and (d) approximation of the cost associated with each of them. In this step, a critical priority analysis is performed on each of the subsystems. The purpose of the analysis is to decide what to do, how to do it, and when to do it.

11. *Prepare a multiyear plan*. A three- to five-year plan for developing a comprehensive library MIS is recommended. However, if an MIS is not in place during the introduction of strategic planning, one should be developed concurrently with the planning process.

12. *Conduct continuous review and annual recycle*. The planning process for an effective MIS does not stop. Because of the dynamic factors involved in a library participating in strategic planning, the purpose and objective of a total MIS effort must be constantly reviewed, tested, and refreshed. Each year, the planning steps should be recycled. The structure of the total MIS should be reviewed in light of changes occurring within the library. Eldin and Croft say "these changes may remove the requirements for some subsystems, or may require the addition of subsystems. The priority analysis should be re-done to reflect any changes."[2]

THE COMPUTER AND THE MIS

The need for computer technology with MIS depends on the size of the library. A small public library may be able to handle its information for strategic planning without a computer. On the other hand, a large public library (e.g., 200 employees and a multi-million dollar budget) would be well-advised to use a computer. With the abundance of micro- and mini-computers, it is now much easier to have access to this valuable technology than it was a decade ago. Eldin and Croft explain the computer's relationship to an MIS this way:

In the strictest sense, it would be possible for an MIS to exist without the use of a computer; however, the time and manpower used to maintain such a system would soon grow out of all proportions. As organizations become more and more complex, everyone cannot be up-to-date on all aspects of the operations. Without some kind of summary or exception procedure, managers could not operate effectively. Processing of data and information becomes vital to their decision making. To maintain a data bank manually with all of the necessary information and the desired degree of currency is nearly impossible. Combined with the proper tools and techniques, the use of the computer greatly simplifies this task. It provides management with the essential elements of information that have been objectively assessed, a necessity for effective decision making.[3]

WHY AN MIS FAILS

Due to the inability of MIS designers to foresee all requirements, there have been more failures than successes with MIS.[4] An effective computer MIS has five elements: (1) a database with multiple files; (2) various functionally adjacent applications, such as inventory control; (3) an information-retrieval system, which allows for management reports at will; (4) simulation capability; and (5) online access to the database.

Organizations that have been unable to get these five elements to produce an effective system have failed, according to Coleman and Riley, primarily because:

1. Their database was difficult to build on a modular basis, file by file, without interrupting the daily flow of activities.
2. The adjacent applications were too difficult and costly to design and redesign.
3. The simulation capability required data factors that were neither built in nor available as needed.[5]

Library planners need to keep in mind the difference between what is theoretically possible in an MIS and what can be done in practical terms. In theory, it is possible to visualize a computerized databank in which every scrap of management information available to the library, whether internally or externally generated, may be stored, and subsequently used on demand for strategic planning activities. Such concepts normally sort out the data by level of detail and length of time required, on the basis that information for strategic decisions must cover a longer time period, but in much less detail than information required for day-to-day operations.

Other reasons MIS fail are:

- They are inflexible. Changes and new subsystems cannot be incorporated into the MIS without major overhauling and revamping.
- Adequate training sessions are not held for library managers who need to use MIS. If managers do not understand how to use the MIS, they will ignore it.

- MIS have been oriented and designed more in terms of the computer than the user.
- They do not contain sufficient control measures and evaluation criteria.
- They use unreliable and undependable sources for input data.
- Information gleaned from an MIS is not distinguishable between what is to be used for strategic planning and that to be used for operational purposes.

IMPLEMENTATION

After bottlenecks in the information flow have been removed and there has been a melding of the subsystems in the MIS, implementation is the next step. Resistance to change will be one of the major obstacles to overcome during implementation of MIS. The library director has to take the lead in reducing resistance to change and encouraging acceptance of the MIS. S/he has to create the proper organizational environment and provide opportunities for library managers to engage in MIS training and development programs. Furthermore, it is imperative that the director support the MIS program. If the director gives little or no attention to MIS, then the other managers may feel little enthusiasm for it and, consequently, it will be infrequently used.

For implementing an MIS involving technology, Murdick and Ross provide a list of tasks and responsibilities that have to be completed:

1. Organizing the personnel for implementation.
2. Acquiring and laying out facilities and offices.
3. Developing procedures for installation and testing.
4. Developing the training program for operating personnel.
5. Completing the system's hardware.
6. Acquiring required hardware.
7. Designing forms.
8. Generating files.
9. Completing cutover to a new system.
10. Obtaining acceptance.
11. Testing the entire system.
12. Providing system maintenance (debugging and improving).[6]

During the design and implementation of MIS, there is the danger of placing too little emphasis on what management is and giving too much attention to the system's technology. The missing efforts have resulted from a failure to develop a clear and precise understanding of the manner in which the information-system output will benefit the library manager.

REFERENCES

1. William R. King and David I. Cleland, *Strategic Planning and Policy* (New York: Van Nostrand Reinhold, 1978), p. 222.
2. Hamed K. Eldin and F. Max Croft, *Information Systems: A Management Science Approach* (New York: Petrocelli Books, 1974), pp. 53–54.
3. Eldin and Croft, p. 46.
4. Frederik H. Lutter, "Why MIS Is No Hit," *Administrative Management* 31 (December 1970): 12.
5. Raymond J. Coleman and M. J. Riley, *MIS: Management Dimensions* (San Francisco, CA: Holden-Day, Inc., 1973), p. 9.
6. Robert G. Murdick and Joel E. Ross, *Information Systems for Modern Management* (Englewood Cliffs, NJ: Prentice-Hall, 1971), p. 508.

9

STRATEGIC PLANNING AND PPBS

❝Management is, in the end, the most creative of all arts — for its medium is human talent itself. **❞**

—Robert S. McNamara

This book would be incomplete without a discussion of the Planning-Programming-Budgeting System (PPBS). Strategic planning and PPBS have many common characteristics. Of all of the various management systems and techniques, PPBS is most closely related to strategic planning.

Other management systems, such as Program Evaluation and Review Technique (PERT), Management by Objectives (MBO), and Zero-Base Budgeting (ZBB), are all commendable in their own unique ways, but their comprehensiveness can be questioned. None of them possesses *all* management aspects, principles, and potential applications to libraries.

However, principles of PERT, MBO, and ZBB can be effectively used as subunits of the library's overall strategic planning system. For example, in 1961, when PERT was brought into the vocabulary of forward-thinking managers, it was, as it is today, believed that efficient management must always stem from a precise statement of an objective; that any project must begin with an explicit definition of what is to be achieved. Decisions need to be made regarding what are the critical (important) and noncritical jobs. An organization such as a library, with its various routine tasks, could apply principles of PERT toward improvement of efficiency.

MBO is a way to manage libraries by identifying objectives and applying them as criteria to judge the quality and effectiveness of inputs and activities. A high priority is placed on defining the library's objectives and communicating them to all library personnel. The "systems management-oriented" conceptualization of MBO is much closer to PPBS and strategic planning than is its "human relations-oriented" concept. MBO may be considered a subset of strategic planning.

ZBB demands close examination of all existing and proposed new programs. While the conceptual framework of ZBB is unassailable, it still remains unproven, especially at the level of strategic resource allocation. In addition, ZBB, PERT, and MBO devote little attention to the important conceptual and operational aspects of strategy. Moreover, PPBS and strategic planning permit a formalized structure for pursuing objectives through a strategy that is implemented through a series of output-oriented programs.

WHAT IS PPBS?

Hartley defines the Planning-Programming-Budgeting System as:

> A conceptual approach to decision making developed by the RAND Corporation and installed in the Department of Defense in 1961; a structured procedure for policy determination; introduced into the entire federal establishment in 1965; emphasized outputs, program activities, and accomplishments; long-range planning, analytic evaluative tools, and economic rationality are basic ingredients.[1]

PPBS involves a detailed phase-by-phase checking of progress in program development. At each important interval, programs are assessed in terms of past accomplishments and probability of success. PPBS, with its output focus and its input-output relationship, can provide a library with a powerful vehicle for showing what results it is accomplishing and how it is accomplishing them. It can provide substantial assistance to a decision maker by displaying library goals and alternative means for achieving them, including both the benefits and costs of each alternative. When resources are limited, a PPBS can assist with more effective allocation and management. PPBS is being rediscovered by libraries and other service agencies in the 1980s.

What distinguishes PPBS from other management techniques is that its elements are interrelated. The planning and programming dimensions are interdependent and, when combined with the budgeting dimension, a unified system is formulated. Failure to implement one part of the system will have an effect on the other parts.

PPBS modernizes library management and decision making at all levels in a variety of ways. It works as an integrated system to improve the information base for policy, programs, and resource-allocation decisions. It is a verifying and comparing process for higher-level review and analysis of program alternatives. It provides, through narrative and numerical expression, an explicit determination of the relative efficiency and economy of allocating limited resources to alternate plans for achieving concrete objectives. Also, like strategic planning, it is a means for revealing the long-range consequences (in terms of estimated costs and benefits) of annual or short-range decisions and actions for library plans, programs, and resource allocations.

The program budgeting and systems analysis components of PPBS can be traced in American industry to the 1920s when General Motors and Du Pont formulated working documents whose purpose was to identify major objectives, to define programs essential to these goals, to identify resources and to relate them to specific types of objectives, and to analyze systematically the alternatives available. The general public first became aware of PPBS when Charles Hitch of the RAND Corporation became comptroller of the U.S. Defense Department and introduced the system for Defense Secretary Robert McNamara. Prior to the use of PPBS, the Department of Defense did not have an integrated mission-oriented system for planning and allocating its resources.

The experience of PPBS in the Department of Defense prompted President Lyndon B. Johnson to decide that the PPBS approach should be applied to the other departments and agencies of the executive branch of the federal government. On August 25, 1965, Johnson announced his decision:

> This morning I have just concluded a breakfast meeting with the Cabinet and with the heads of Federal agencies and I am asking each of them to immediately begin to introduce a very new and very revolutionary system of planning and programming and budgeting throughout the vast Federal government, so that through the tools of modern management the full promise of a finer life can be brought to every American at the lowest possible cost. This program is designed to achieve three major objectives. It will help us to find new ways to do jobs faster, to do jobs better, and to do jobs less expensively.[2]

Prior to the government's commitment to PPBS, the federal budget, according to Anshen, did not provide the necessary information to:

1. Choose among alternative goals when available resources are not sufficient to undertake the achievement of all goals concurrently.
2. Measure the total immediate cost of activities designed to achieve any single goal.
3. Identify currently the implicit future costs of present program decisions.
4. Chart with confidence the probable future course of the expenditure side of the budget in total and significant detail.
5. Evaluate the efficiency and effectiveness of the performance of ongoing programs by comparing costs with achievements.[3]

Traditional budgeting did not pay much attention to the goals and objectives of programs for which the government committed resources. Neither was there much concern with alternatives or better ways for achieving program objectives. The absence of alternatives and the lack of information needed for judging the effect of either an increase or decrease in funding level of a given program had led to the situation in which the judgment of the Bureau of the Budget staffs had, at times, to replace arbitrarily the judgment of those who knew much more about the program.

OBJECTIVES OF PPBS

One objective of PPBS is to specify and clarify the goals and objectives of a library's programs. Unless a library is aware of what its programs are intended to do, it becomes difficult to know whether such programs are serving their purposes. PPBS, in this respect, has the effect of impelling libraries to take stock of what they are doing and to chart their course accordingly.

Being output-oriented, PPBS is interested in the relation between the output of a specific library program and its objectives. Only when the output of a specific library program is analyzed in the context of its objective does it become meaningful. Such analysis is also the basis for determining the effectiveness of a program.

PPBS aims toward planning programs for the first year and subsequent years. Planning is long-range and considers the multiyear implications of current decisions. This aspect of PPBS is identified with the *planning* element in strategic planning. Another similarity found in both systems is that planning and programming normally use a three- to five-year forward time horizon. The time horizon, however, is dependent upon the PPBS being considered. Nevertheless, the first future year of PPBS is the detailed budget year.

Another aim of the PPBS is to use analysis in the search for the best, most cost-effective alternatives for accomplishing the objectives of library programs. Under PPBS, programs come under periodic review to ensure that library resources are used to the best advantage.

An overall objective of PPBS for library management is to integrate the planning, programming, and budgeting functions of a library into a formal system. The system would provide better information on a library's objectives and alternative ways to attain them, including explicit presentation of the costs and benefits of the alternatives. The primary aim is to assist administrators in improving their decision making in the areas of resource allocation and management. PPBS also creates a decision-making environment in which the basis of competition among subordinate organizational units in a library is the effectiveness of subordinate unit contributions to the library's overall goals.

■■■ INTERRELATED DIMENSIONS OF PPBS ■■■

The three major dimensions of the PPBS acronym are: planning, programming, and budgeting. It cannot be emphasized too much that these three dimensions are not separate dimensions but are interrelated and interdependent.

Novick makes it clear that "planning and programming are really aspects of the same process."[4] Programming is the more specific determination of courses of action (i.e., strategies) generated from planning. Plans are translated into programs. De Ganaro defined the three dimensions in the following manner: (1) planning—the study of objectives and alternative ways to achieve objectives, of future environments, and of contingencies and how to respond to them; (2) programming—a method of describing activities according to objectives or outputs and of relating these objectives to the costs or inputs needed to produce the outputs or effectiveness desired; and (3) budgeting—the activity through which funds are requested, appropriated, apportioned and accounted.[5]

Finally, PPBS is the structure within which the planning, programming, and budgeting take place. Perhaps it would be more accurate to state that the *system* in PPBS is the process of planning, programming, and budgeting.

MAJOR COMPONENTS OF PPBS

To present PPBS as a formal system in libraries, it is necessary to understand its four major components. The four components, with brief descriptions, are: (1) program structure—this component describes the framework of the system with its objectives; three levels of classification (i.e., categories, subcategories, and elements) are used in composing a complete program structure; (2) program memoranda—a comparison of characteristics of each alternative given for obtaining the objectives make up the document known as the program memoranda; (3) program financial plan—this document contains a continuing record from year to year of the outputs, costs, and financing of all agency programs; it reflects the multi-year programs of a library by summarizing the past, the current, and subsequent budgetary years; and (4) special analytic studies—studies supply the analytic foundation for decisions made in the program memoranda. Part or all of program issues may be exposed to analytic studies in order to enhance the decision-making process. Special analytic studies may also be called cost-effectiveness, cost-benefit analysis, or systems analysis. Whatever they are called, their basic thrust is to provide a quantifiable evaluation of alternatives for the library.

The four PPBS components have been followed as a formal system structure very closely by the various federal government agencies. However, many other agencies (e.g., state governments, libraries) which have supposedly operated in the PPBS mode have attempted to create their own structure and, consequently, they are lacking the basic ingredients and philosophical foundation of an effective PPBS.

ADVANTAGES OF PPBS

Many advantages for libraries are inherent in the PPBS. One of them is that it operates as a zero-base budgeting process. Zero-base budgeting differs from incremental budgeting in that it reviews and justifies each library program beginning from zero, while incremental budgeting operates on the basis of a percent or actual dollar increment over the present period. With PPBS, continuation of each program is questioned and must be documented; this approach encourages reallocation of funds to new programs when old programs cannot be fully justified or when better use of library resources is identified.

PPBS is an approach to decision making that systematically integrates all aspects of planning. A three-dimensioned procedure (e.g., alternatives, program elements, and time) may be illustrated to reveal how each program element in PPBS is multidimensional in respect to the contribution it makes to the library program. Many management systems lack the integrating and systematic approach offered by PPBS.

WHAT PPBS IS NOT

PPBS is not a decision-making process that can be conducted on a computer. Decisions will continue to come from the political process, influenced by value judgments, and result from the pressures coming from the various interested parties as well as from the process of systematic analysis.

It is not a system that promotes centralized decision making for the library. However, centralization could result from using PPBS because superior analytical and informational technologies present a library manager with the opportunity to exercise more control.

PPBS does not imply that the entire output of a library can be quantified and measured. Many products gleaned from a PPBS may be nonquantifiable but extremely valuable. It is not limited to cost accounting and to economic consideration in the narrow sense.

Furthermore, PPBS is not a substitute for the experience, intuition, and judgment of the library decision makers. On the contrary, its objective is to sharpen that intuition and judgment by stating library programs more precisely, by discovering new alternatives, and by making explicit the comparison among alternatives.[6]

STRATEGIES AND PPBS

The formulation of strategies is a crucial part of the PPBS developmental and implementation process. It is mandatory that strategic variables in the planning component of PPBS be carefully compared and reviewed independently of one another. Strategies for alternatives must be ranked in order of importance and timing. Moreover, all strategies must relate explicitly back to a well-developed program structure. Using the principles of PPBS with strategic planning, library managers can operate from a stance that encompasses formality, practicality, alternate paths, developed courses of action, and annual reviews of ongoing activities and programs.

SIMILARITIES BETWEEN PPBS AND STRATEGIC PLANNING

While strategic planning devotes much more emphasis to a library's mission, goals, objectives, and strategy formulation than does PPBS, the two management systems do share several parallels. Steiner summarizes the similarities:

> Both are concerned with making better current decisions in light of future environmental forces; both involve participation of people; both are recycled about once a year; both are directed at achieving stated objectives; both are conceived as being managerial learning processes; both run into comparable problems in application (e.g., demanding too much time of managers, delegating too much planning responsibility to staff, generating paperwork, or complicating communications between managers and staff experts); and both must operate in an atmosphere charged with political considerations.[7]

REFERENCES

1. Harry J. Hartley, *Educational Planning-Programming-Budgeting: A Systems Approach* (Englewood Cliffs, NJ: Prentice-Hall, 1968), p. 256.

2. David Novick, *Program Budgeting: Program Analysis and the Federal Budget* (New York: Holt, Rinehart, and Winston, 1967), p. xix.

3. Melvin Anshen, "The Federal Budget as an Instrument for Management and Analysis," in *Program Budgeting,* ed. David Novick (Cambridge, MA: Harvard University Press, 1965), p. 14.

4. David Novick, ed., "The Department of Defense," in *Program Budgeting* (Washington, DC: Government Printing Office, 1964).

5. George J. De Ganaro, *A Planning-Programming-Budgeting System (PPBS) in Academic Libraries: Development of Objectives and Effectiveness Measures* (Unpublished doctoral dissertation, University of Florida, 1971), p. 30.

6. Donald E. Riggs, *An Application of a Planning-Programming-Budgeting System to a Technical Services Processing Center* (Unpublished doctoral dissertation, Virginia Polytechnic Institute and State University, 1975), pp. 17–25.

7. George A. Steiner, *Strategic Planning: What Every Manager Must Know* (New York: Free Press, 1979), pp. 328–29.

10

THE SYSTEMS APPROACH

❝I keep six honest serving men (They taught me all I know); Their names are What and Why and When and How and Where and Who. ❞
—Rudyard Kipling

According to Churchman, a "system" is a set of parts coordinated to accomplish a set of goals.[1] In addition to coordinating parts, a system provides harmony among its systematic activities. Some believe that a system is more than the sum of its parts. It is analytic and can depict abstractions from reality. It can also be empirical in nature, since observed interactions may be viewed as a system.

One intention of this chapter is to reveal how the concept of systems approach is beneficial to the strategic planning process. The systems approach assists with maintaining the coordination of actions among the interdependent subsystems (e.g., cataloging, acquisitions) of a library (a system) that may be affected by the implementation of strategic planning. A plan to introduce a major computer project into the library system, for example, would have a direct impact on many of the subsystems throughout the library.

Since "everything depends on everything else" in the library, the systems approach to strategic library planning is complicated. Nearly all subsystems of a library are interdependent. All of these interacting and interconnecting subsystems form a unified whole (or system). To add further complexity to "systems," the library itself may be perceived as being a "subsystem" of a larger system (e.g., a city government, a university). Planning itself may also be viewed as a system and, within the planning system, one will find subsystems.

SYSTEMS ANALYSIS

The concept of systems analysis may be defined as a systematic way of identifying and ordering the different components, relationships, processes, and other properties of a system or subsystem. Its purpose is to evaluate the system in terms of accuracy, efficiency, effectiveness, economy, and timeliness. An additional purpose may be that of designing a new or improved system. The design should eliminate or minimize deficiencies and improve the overall library operations. Carlsen and Lewis deduce that the person(s) who performs the analysis should be concerned with (1) assessing the current situation, (2) developing a method for what should be done, and (3) planning for the new design's application and for implementation of the system.[2]

Systems analysis provides a framework in which to look at each component of the strategic planning process. Alternative action plans must be available to the library manager while s/he is working in the decision-making mode. These alternative plans should be derived from careful analysis, not merely from subjective judgment or intuition. The decision maker uses both qualitative and quantitative measures in a logical manner when reducing the large components of an abstract problem to a manageable, more simplified form.

Rational strategic decisions result from following the conceptual framework for analysis. The conceptual framework for systems analysis is not a panacea which will solve all strategic planning problems. On the contrary, it sometimes raises more questions than it solves; it can be argued that these questions are more apt to be the right ones than those that might be raised without the systems approach. The essential appeal of the conceptual framework is that it is descriptive of the way in which everyone knows s/he should, or thinks that s/he does, make decisions. According to Cleland and King, its value is that it forces the library manager to give proper attention to enumerating the alternative strategies, the entire range of contingencies, and the scope of possible outcomes in a fashion that would be impractical if the problem were approached at an intuitive or informal level.[3]

Administrators have to use caution and not assume that strategic planning is based solely on analysis. Even though analysis is extremely important in strategic planning, one should not overlook the value of synthesis. Library managers are responsible for putting together the disparate parts and developing a plan that is practical and functional. Synthesis enables creative managers to visualize new relationships among the different elements in a strategic plan.

SYSTEMS MODELS

The complexities of planning can be reduced by using models. Systems models can be constructed to provide a general framework in which strategic planning can be assessed. Models can be depicted as graphs and as mathematical or computer-output configurations; they can simulate real library events or transactions and they can be used to predict the consequence of actions or strategies that are being contemplated during the planning process. All in all, systems models are more useful for library managers in diagnosing and analysis than for choosing among planning alternatives.

For example, systems modeling could be performed by a public library before it decides on when, where, and how to build a new branch library. Some factors to include in the modeling of a proposed branch library would be: (1) population of the area to be served, (2) expected usage of the new facility, (3) site selection, (4) costs of construction/equipment/personnel, (5) development of an opening day collection, (6) use of modern technology, and (7) dependence on central library for administration, policy, and centralized processing of materials. Each of these factors could be modeled to unearth practical alternatives. Through the process of suboptimizing (i.e., integrating the conceptual framework with the practicalities of the real library world), library managers would be able to choose the best alternative from the ''subsystems'' brought forth for the modeled components of the branch library. It would be helpful to construct a matrix displaying the relationships among the modeled components of the branch library and the working relationship between the branch library and the central library.

A garden-variety model can yield more opportunities to view library operations on a more practical basis than would a highly scientific model. The branch library model and submodels permit the strategic planning team to gain a perspective on how the branch library would be developed and how it would fit into the total library system. After the branch library is completed and ready for service, the planning team can reflect on how well the planning model matches the real thing.

Attempting to model variables in the library's external environment is difficult. Guessing what impact political forces will have on library funding for a new branch library will depend more on practical knowledge of how the voters feel about additional taxes than on a model. The mood of the voters regarding a library bond/levy cannot be "modeled" with any degree of certainty. However, polls taken by scientific sampling of the voters can provide perceptions that should be given consideration by the planning team.

Frequently used models in library systems analysis include those that are associated with cost-benefit or general economic concerns. An academic library could use the cost-benefit model while considering the possibilities of gaining more space for an expanding collection when the prospects for new construction funds are nil. Such a model would include alternative plans: for example, the use of moveable, compact shelving in the main university library to acquire additional space for the collection in the same square footage. A model could be constructed for an alternative involving the storage of little-used books in an accessible warehouse on campus. Application of the systems approach to the alternative for space would likely include the following components: (1) degree of user access to the collection, (2) maintenance costs of a warehouse storage facility, (3) renovation of the storage facility (e.g., making provision for proper climatic conditions), (4) staff requirements for retrieving books from the storage facility, (5) capital expenditures for compact shelving, (6) browsing versus closed access to the collection, and (7) future space needs.

Several submodels can be used in the systems approach involving library costs and benefits. To be useful, submodels must directly relate to the comprehensive model for a specific library issue. For example, a model for collection development could include submodels for current fiction, approval plans, subject specialists/bibliographers, retrospective acquisitions, serials, microforms, and resource sharing. A submodel encompasses a set of entities that are changing, and they include a mix of various library resources. Prudent library managers will put the feasible submodels together to form a functional, unified whole (model).

The primary value of modeling is to develop a basis for the manager to predict future library events. The abstraction of reality gained from modeling is a valuable planning tool. However, managers have to acknowledge that models cannot be used for all strategic planning library issues and problems. The models essentially represent a way to approach particular challenges and subprograms which are or will be important parts of the library's overall strategic planning process. Models will enhance library effectiveness by predicting the effect of change on the performance of the entire library system.

A SYSTEM OF PLANS

The output of the planning process is a set of decisions concerning mission, strategy, goals, objectives, etc. These decisions are reflected in the plan—or the documentary output of planning. However, for a sophisticated organization like a library, the plan cannot be a simple entity. Rather, it is a *system* of interrelated and interdependent sub-plans which reflect the various dimensions of the environments being faced, the opportunities that exist, the relevant organizational clientele groups, and interrelationships among these elements.

The illustration on the next page depicts a hierarchical relationship among the mission statement, conceptual goals, and operational objectives. The mission statement is an abstract statement describing the general purpose of the library. Project plans are derived from conceptual goals that are stated in unspecific terms; however, the goals and plans must be attainable. Operational objectives are contingent on conceptual goals; plans evolving from operational objectives are usually very specific and normally are to be achieved within a determined short-range time period.

All of the various plans are interrelated and form a system of plans that can be used to guide the library. These plans document the planning endeavor within the library and provide the basis for communicating goals, objectives, and strategies throughout the library system. The plans should contain a "coping element" which would enable the library to grow, refine, and continually undergo constructive change; this is the purpose of a strategic planning process. The formulation of strategies has to be based on the interrelationships of all three phases (subplans) of the total plan. As Alfred North Whitehead has said, "To be is to be related."

The following illustration reflects the relationships among sub-plans in a system of plans:

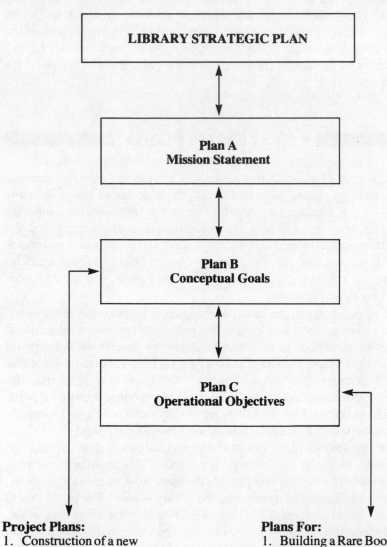

Project Plans:
1. Construction of a new library.
2. Introduction of a new computing system.
3. Obtain funding for a conservation program.

Plans For:
1. Building a Rare Book room in new library.
2. Implementing an online circulation control system within nine months.
3. Deacidifying 2,000 books in one year.

DECISION MAKING

A primary reason for using the systems approach in the strategic planning process is to enhance decision making. "The most common source of mistakes in management decisions is emphasis on finding the right answers rather than the right questions," according to Peter Drucker. Which goals, objectives, strategies, and alternatives shall be selected will depend, to a large extent, on the information gleaned from the systems. Strategies, for example, are formulated after reviewing information derived from rational decision making which translates missions into goals and subsequently establishes major objectives and plans of action to achieve the goals.

The decision-making process contains the following components:

- Gathering information.
- Analyzing information.
- Using performance appraisals.
- Examining models (How will the system behave? What variables will affect the system?).
- Formulating strategies and considering practical alternatives.
- Forecasting the end results of strategies.
- Listing criteria for alternative selection.
- Selecting alternative(s).

After the appropriate alternative is selected, the decision is implemented. The above components are arranged in sequential order with information being the key to the entire process. If new information develops after implementation has begun, library managers may have to return to an earlier step in the decision-making process and reassess that step and subsequent steps that led to the decision. Information is crucial, and it must be complete, relevant, and timely.

Strategic planning must always be concerned with concurrent and interdependent decisions that have an impact on the selection of future directions for the library. These decisions may refer to completely new ventures for the library or to the continuation of existing programs. They constitute arenas in which opportunities for fulfillment of the goals of the library may arise or in which threats to that fulfillment may be encountered.

REFERENCES

1. C. West Churchman, *The Systems Approach* (New York: Delacorte Press, 1968), p. 29.

2. Robert D. Carlsen and James A. Lewis, *The Systems Analysis Workbook: A Complete Guide to Project Implementation and Control* (Englewood Cliffs, NJ: Prentice-Hall, 1973), p. 19.

3. David I. Cleland and William R. King, *Systems Analysis and Project Management* (New York: McGraw-Hill, 1975), pp. 93–94.

C H A P T E R

11

IMPLEMENTATION OF STRATEGIC PLANNING

❝Strategic planning without effective implementation is little more than a misplaced academic drill.❞

—James B. Whittaker

The previous chapters in this book encompass much of the preparatory work for implementing strategic planning. This chapter provides an overview of issues that the library manager needs to consider before and during actual implementation. The implementation process permits the manager the opportunity to instigate and complete organizational change in the library.

ORGANIZATIONAL COMPLEXITIES

Like other human organizations, the library is complex. It comprises an intricate personnel structure and a number of interdependent subsystems (e.g., acquisitions, cataloging, reference). Managers are charged with getting high performance from their subordinates and administering their assigned areas with top-level efficiency and quality effectiveness. Strategic planning is geared to assist the manager with his/her duties and responsibilities and in achieving goals and objectives. However, the implementation of strategic planning brings with it modifications in the organizational fabric of the library. For example, resources may be redeployed, job assignments may be enlarged, and departments may be expanded or merged.

Change

Since change contains an element of the unknown, nearly everyone has some apprehension about changing from the current way of doing things to a new way. The greatest difficulty in instituting change, be it change involving new ways of doing things, new ways of making choices, or new library services, does not lie in the design and development of the changes themselves. Rather, according to King and Cleland, the greatest obstructions to positive change lie in the processes that are used to implement them.[1]

The best way to encourage the library staff members to accept change is to let them have a say in constructing and implementing it. Besse provides a set of guidelines that will help make staff more agreeable to changes required in the implementation of strategic planning:

1. Change is more acceptable when it is understood than when it is not.
2. Change is more acceptable when it does not threaten security than when it does.
3. Change is more acceptable when those affected have helped to create it than when it has been externally imposed.
4. Change is more acceptable when it results from an application of previously established impersonal principles than it is when it is dictated by personal order.
5. Change is more acceptable when it follows a series of successful changes than it is when it follows a series of failures.

6. Change is more acceptable when it is inaugurated after prior change has been assimilated than when it is inaugurated during the confusion of other major change.
7. Change is more acceptable if it has been planned than it is if it is experimental.
8. Change is more acceptable to people new on a job than to people old on the job.
9. Change is more acceptable to people who share in the benefits of change than to those who do not.
10. Change is more acceptable if the organization has been trained to plan for improvement than it is if the organization is accustomed to static procedures.[2]

Positive Attitude

The primary initial goal of the implementation process should be the achievement of a positive attitude change, if it does not already exist, about strategic planning. Training seminars and workshops are excellent vehicles for instilling positive attitudes.

Library management study teams can be used to work on specific areas of strategic planning. These teams can conduct training seminars to increase planning knowledge and to design details of the implementation process. Such seminars, in addition to aiding the overall educational process on implementation, can particularly lead to the following contributions:

- A greater commitment to strategic planning.
- An improvement in the library managers' knowledge of planning.
- Identification of the library's weaknesses and ways for correcting them.
- Realization of an overall, positive attitudinal change regarding strategic planning and its implementation.

Motivation

In an organizational context, motivation is the managerial stimulation of employees to accomplish the goals and objectives of the library. This is done by creating an environment in which the employee can satisfy his/her needs and, in so doing, participate favorably in implementing the library strategic planning activities. Motivation normally begins with an individual's perception of his/her needs. The library usually provides some need satisfiers (e.g., merit compensation for outstanding job performance).

The library director can play a signal role in motivating employees. S/he can give special recognition to members of the planning team; further, the director can motivate the participants by articulating the importance of his/her own commitment to strategic planning. Motivation is the essential ingredient for making implementation successful.

A PLAN FOR IMPLEMENTING PLANNING

After the primary components of strategic planning have been identified and delineated and the organizational complexities have been given serious consideration, it is then time to develop a plan for implementing planning. The plan is the only way to ensure that the necessary activities are performed. It should include these aspects:

- *Documentation of responsibilities*. The library director is ultimately responsible for the stategic planning process and all of its activities. Nevertheless, there is no way that the director can perform all of the responsibilities associated with the planning process. Each member of the planning team needs to know, in writing, precisely what his/her responsibilities are. Written clarification of each planning team member's assigned activities will be beneficial to the entire planning effort. Overlapping performances, omission of vital planning procedures, and possibilities of unstructured events occurring will be minimized with responsibilities being documented.
- *Use of responsibility charts*. The director is likely to use responsibility charts to assist the planning team in seeing what each member is doing to achieve the goals and objectives. The chart will include the names of the person(s) designated as having primary responsibility for a specific goal. The objective to be achieved will be given, and the strategy's number and description will be listed. Moreover, the strategic steps to be followed will be given with the starting and completion dates.

Following is an example of a responsibility chart:

RESPONSIBILITY CHART		
Goal Number _____ Title _____		
Objective Number _____ Title _____		
Strategy Number _____ Title _____		
Name of Planning Team Member _____		
Date _____		
Strategic Steps	Start Date	Completion Date

A responsibility chart is an excellent management tool to use during the implementation period. It serves as a constant reminder to the planning team member responsible for carrying out strategic planning and helps ensure that planning becomes a working process, not something that is imaginary or theoretical.

It is not mandatory to use a responsibility chart and, if one is used, it can be constructed according to what the planning team deems most appropriate for its library. Also, there can be different types of responsibility charts used by a library. After the charts are agreed upon and prepared, each planning team member and the director should receive copies. The charts will permit the entire team to see who is doing what and when the strategic steps are to be completed.

• *Setting up activity charts.* In addition to the responsibility charts, each planning participant should maintain activity charts. These charts can be very useful for the individual departments. The charts permit the planners to check on the progress of a given activity or task; however, it does not have to be a complex instrument. Following is an example:

ACTIVITY CHART

Activity	Start Date		Completion Date	
	Planned	Actual	Planned	Actual

• *Scheduling of the planning cycle.* The length of time it takes to complete the "first time around" planning cycle will vary, depending on the size of the library. Some of the planning steps (e.g., strategy formulation) will require more time than other steps. Further, it takes time to "think through" the pertinent information assembled, and the planning team members will normally be busy with their regular duties and responsibilities. Even the smallest library engaging in strategic planning should allow at least six months to work through the entire cycle. An example of a one-year planning cycle chart follows:

ONE-YEAR PLANNING CYCLE CHART

	Sept.	Oct.	Nov.	Dec.	Jan.	Feb.	Mar.	Apr.	May	June	July	Aug.
Mission	■											
Goals		■										
Objectives			■									
Strategy Formulation					■	■	■					
Alternatives & Contingencies								■				
Policies									■			
Resource Allocation										■		
Evaluation											■	
Adjustments												■

The planning cycle chart is to be used in conjunction with the planning processes described in the other chapters. Again, this chart is an example only; each library will have to tailor a chart for its own planning needs.

Before beginning the planning cycle, a sufficient number of introductory meetings must be held with the planning team. Everyone on the team needs to know what strategic planning entails, the amount of time required, and the advantages to be gained from it. As explained in the earlier part of this book, the library director must serve as the leader throughout the planning process. The success of the implementation process will depend on the director's leadership and commitment to strategic planning.

THE ONGOING PLANNING TEAM

Along with the leadership of the library director, the ongoing planning team constitutes the most important component of the strategic planning process. The planning team's importance lies not only in its expertise, but in its continuation as essentially an intact, working group which is involved with the annual recycling of strategic planning implementation.

Palmour et al. describe the tasks of the group, over the continuing cycles, as:

1. Meeting at regular intervals.
2. Reviewing progress in implementation of strategies and recommending changes or new strategies as necessary.
3. Monitoring experimental strategies aimed at serving target groups and making recommendations about future strategies.
4. Determining the information required to evaluate system performance and designating personnel responsible for its collection.
5. Arranging for periodic input from citizens, library users, and staff and data concerning changes in environment and population.
6. Ensuring adequate dissemination of data collected to maximize utilization and to prevent unnecessary duplication of effort.
7. Examining resource allocations.
8. Evaluating progress, reviewing goals, objectives, and priorities, and modifying the plan as necessary at regular intervals.[3]

REFERENCES

1. William R. King and David I. Cleland, *Strategic Planning and Policy* (New York: Van Nostrand Reinhold, 1978), p. 325.

2. Ralph M. Besse, "Company Planning Must Be Planned," *Dun's Review and Modern Industry* 66 (April 1957): 62–63.

3. Vernon E. Palmour et al., *A Planning Process for Public Libraries* (Chicago: American Library Association, 1980), p. 83.

CHAPTER

12

PLANNING EVALUATION AND CONTROL

66The reward of a thing well done, is to have done it.**99**

—*Ralph Waldo Emerson*

Unquestionably, "designing" and "implementing" are very important components of the strategic planning process. However, good planning will not simply evolve from these two components. To be recognized as effective planning, the process must be evaluated and controlled. If not, the planning activity will not reflect direction and focus. Good intentions of the planning team must be translated into reality.

Evaluating and controlling a library's strategic planning activity is a complex endeavor. Reasons for this include: (1) libraries contain several systems and subsystems. Each of these systems and subsystems will likely have its own evaluation and control mechanism which must be considered during planning for the entire library. (2) A volatile environment may cause results to be far less than planned. Should the planning process be rated poorly because of uncontrollable events? (3) A change in key personnel may cause substantial modifications in planned strategies. Sufficient time may not be available in the current planning cycle to match the new personnel with the already designed and operative strategies.

King and Cleland emphasize the need for planning evaluation and control:

> The concept of planning evaluation and control implies that both the process and results of strategic planning must be evaluated periodically to ask such questions as: What went right? What went wrong? How might our strategic planning process be improved? A planning system that does not have a strategy for review and improvement of the efficiency of strategic-planning efforts in the organization is unlikely to achieve its fullest potential. . . . We stress the importance for planners accepting the need for a philosophy of control to be applied to strategic planning in much the same way that control techniques are applied to the operating activities of the organization. Thus, strategic planning evaluation and control becomes a part of the overall management-control function in the organization. . . . The planning era of the past two decades seems to have led to a degree of "faith" in planning per se which may not be justified. Poor planning may be worse than no planning at all merely because no planning really means an absence of organized planning activities.[1]

WAYS TO EVALUATE

Each library will have to devise ways to evaluate its strategic planning system. Like strategic planning itself, there is no one best evaluation process that can be used in all libraries. Steiner, however, has identified three pertinent questions which can serve as general guidelines while evaluating one's strategic planning system. They are: (1) Are the purposes of the system being achieved? (2) Are requirements of the system being made? and (3) What are some factors that should be included in a comprehensive evaluation survey of a strategic planning system?[2]

In response to question 1, if the purposes of strategic planning are clear and understandable, then it should be possible to assess whether or not the library's strategic planning system is achieving its intent and how well. There can be a multitude of purposes for one's strategic planning system. For example, purposes may include enlarging services offered to the public, turning around the central thrust of the library, or installing an all-encompassing automation program.

In response to question 2, there are several examples in the literature on what is required in a successful strategic planning system. A library's planning system could be measured against those standards that are appropriate for a not-for-profit institution. Schaffir believes that if one or more of the following 10 principles is violated, the planning system will not yield satisfactory results:

1. The planning system must help its authors manage their operations more effectively.
2. The planning system is to establish a mutually agreed upon commitment between the authors of the system and their superior(s).
3. It must contain sufficient information to lend credibility to its promise.
4. It must have strategic focus; that is, it must be part of an overall scheme to accomplish enduring objectives within the context of dynamic, interacting environmental forces.
5. It must foster awareness of options and their likely consequences.
6. It must boil up critical issues, choices, and priorities on which management attention must be focused.
7. It must be linked firmly to the system for allocating and committing funds.
8. It must keep paperwork manageable.
9. It must accommodate a plurality of managerial and planning styles.
10. It must be woven into the fabric of the organization to become a natural part of getting the job done.[3]

Tailoring the strategic planning process to the individual library is an acceptable principle of library management. One cannot avoid special local needs and the contingencies of a specific situational setting of a library. Furthermore, the behavioral styles and competencies of the library managers are due consideration while developing the strategic planning system. However, despite the tailoring approach for each library, there are at least five general ''musts'' that do represent necessary ingredients in the success of a strategic planning process:

1. One of the aims of library management must be that it makes use of a formal planning process as a support to formulate strategic choices.
2. The overall purpose of going through the planning process must be entirely understood at *all* the levels of the library that are involved.
3. There must be at least a minimum of common requirements regarding the standardization of contents, formats, deadlines, methods, etc., of the planning system.
4. The planning system must be integrated with the other management systems of the library (e.g., its management information system).

5. Line managers and department heads must be centrally involved in the planning process.

The above five rules will not ensure that a library's strategic planning process will be successful, but they will definitely enhance the chances.

Finally, it is important to evaluate certain factors of the strategic planning system, as suggested in question 3. Steiner has developed a survey form to be used with profit-making organizations.[4] For the purpose of this book, Steiner's questionnaire has been adapted for use by library managers. The following questionnaire primarily seeks to determine the value library managers attribute to the planning system, whether or not the system produces valuable substantive results, whether or not the system meets the most important standards for a good design, and whether or not the planning processes are effective.

HOW EFFECTIVE IS YOUR LIBRARY'S STRATEGIC PLANNING SYSTEM?

	Not Effective	Very Effective

A. What is the Overall Managerial Perceived Value?

1. The library director believes the system helps him/her to discharge better his/her responsibilities. |___|___|___|___|___|

2. Other major line managers and department heads think the system is useful to them. |___|___|___|___|___|

3. Overall, the benefits of strategic planning are perceived to be greater than the costs by most managers. |___|___|___|___|___|

4. Major changes are needed in our strategic planning system. |___|___|___|___|___|

B. Does Our Strategic Planning System Produce the "Right" Substantive Answers and Results?

5. Developing the basic library mission. |___|___|___|___|___|

6. Foreseeing future major opportunities. |___|___|___|___|___|

7. Foreseeing future major threats. |___|___|___|___|___|

8. Properly appraising the library's strengths. |___|___|___|___|___|

9. Properly appraising the library's weaknesses. |___|___|___|___|___|

Adapted with permission of The Free Press (a division of Macmillan Publishing Co., Inc.) from *Strategic Planning: What Every Manager Must Know* by George A. Steiner. © The Free Press, 1979.

	Not Effective				Very Effective

10. Developing realistic current information.
11. Clarifying priorities.
12. Developing useful long-range goals.
13. Developing useful short-range objectives.
14. Developing realistic strategies.
15. Providing an improvement in services.
16. Preventing unpleasant surprises.
17. Improving performance of personnel.

C. Does Our Planning System Yield Valuable Ancillary Benefits?

18. The system has improved the quality of library management.
19. The system is a unifying, coordinating force in library operations.
20. The system facilitates communications and collaboration throughout the library.

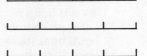

D. What About the Design of the Planning System?

21. The top management of the library has accepted the idea that strategic planning is its major responsibility.
22. Our system fits the management style of our library.
23. The system fits the reality of our strategic decision-making process.
24. The planning committee structure is just right for us.

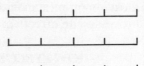

E. Are the Planning Processes Effective?

25. Top management spends an appropriate amount of time on strategic planning.
26. There is too much foot-dragging about planning. More action is needed in place of lip service by the line managers and department heads.
27. Department heads generally spend an appropriate amount of time with other department heads and/or staff in developing strategic plans.
28. The system proceeds on the basis of an acceptable set of procedures.
29. The planning procedures are well understood throughout the library.
30. The work requirement to complete the plans is acceptable to the planning team.

	Not Effective	Very Effective
31. The process is effective in inducing in-depth thinking.		＿＿＿｜＿＿＿｜＿＿＿｜＿＿＿｜
32. Too much attention is paid to putting numbers in boxes. The process is too proceduralized, too routine, too inflexible.		＿＿＿｜＿＿＿｜＿＿＿｜＿＿＿｜
33. New ideas are welcomed.		＿＿＿｜＿＿＿｜＿＿＿｜＿＿＿｜
34. The planning team really faces up to library weaknesses in devising plans.		＿＿＿｜＿＿＿｜＿＿＿｜＿＿＿｜
35. The ability of line managers and department heads to do strategic planning is taken into consideration.		＿＿＿｜＿＿＿｜＿＿＿｜＿＿＿｜

This survey form's usefulness lies in the format it provides for evaluating the accepted design standards and major anticipated results of the planning system. This, in turn, provides a basis for discussion among members of the planning team about shortcomings that should be corrected in the system.

The form will have to be modified to fit the individual library. For instance, it should conform to the interests of different persons on the planning team. Top managers should be asked to evaluate all items in parts A, B, and C, but only selected items in parts D and E.

Overall, the purpose of this questionnaire is to organize thinking about a strategic planning system as a basis for informed and dispassionate discussion of its design and results, with a view toward improving it in terms of perceived managerial needs. The form in its present state, or modified to suit unique situations in a library, appears to do this.

Under part B, questions 5 through 14 are geared toward a mature planning system. Some of these questions are more important than others. For example, questions 12, 13, and 14 are of very high significance because the main focus and purpose of a strategic planning system is to help libraries formulate and implement appropriate goals, objectives, and strategies to meet the changing environment.

It should be remembered that a perfect planning system will not guarantee that management will choose the "right" strategy. But, it can be said that, other things being equal, a library is more likely to develop the "right" strategy with an appropriate strategic planning system than without it. Skilled library managers are more likely to formulate better strategies than are unskilled managers; skilled managers are more likely to develop a strategic planning system than are unskilled managers. Steiner reminds us that good management and effective strategic planning systems go together.[5]

The methods described for evaluating strategic planning systems are by no means perfect. They can, however, assist in identifying areas where a library's strategic planning system needs improvement.

PLANNING CONTROL

As used here, control refers to regulating the activities and outputs of the planning process itself. To control is to constrain activities in harmony with plans that have been established by the planning team. Control action is taken either to change the plan or performance as required.

Although planning, evaluation, and control appear to be three separate activities, they are closely intertwined and cannot exist independently. Zachman states "that if the capability to plan and to evaluate and to control are not all present, the strategic planning system will be ineffective."[6]

Strategic Checkpoints

The planning team should establish strategic points whose primary purpose is to determine if environmental or internal organizational forces have developed to justify continuing a particular course of action, or alternatively, to redirect the strategy. The review of strategic checkpoints should examine strategic alternatives and the present library direction by: (1) checking the credibility of goals, objectives, and supporting strategies by probing into the underlying assumptions and data bases; (2) creating, where necessary, other alternative strategies and goals/objectives for further consideration; and (3) reviewing the effect on the employment of library resources, in relation to the planned resource allocation scheme.

Strategic checkpoints are benchmarks that may be used to control progress toward the fulfillment of a given library strategy. King and Cleland indicate that these benchmarks establish thresholds of the library's organizational performance which, if met, establish the validity of a given strategy.[7]

Consistency

There must be consistency in all control mechanisms and activities. Fluctuating among different control systems while assessing a single strategy will lead to havoc.

Consistency will strengthen the strategic planning process by ensuring that a given strategy would attempt to maximize external opportunities and internal strengths and to minimize external threats and internal weaknesses. In essence, this is the test of consistency. Unfortunately, while it is common to aspire to a strategic equation which incorporates the best of all worlds for the library, this is not always possible.

The planning team has to be consistent in its reporting of findings, data collection for similar library areas, strategy formulation, record keeping, and conformity with previous practices. Coordination among the various library departments during the creation of strategy will be much easier if there is consistency in interdepartmental relationships.

⬚ Short-Range versus Long-Range Planning ⬚

Library managers are, by nature, action-oriented. They, like managers in other fields, want to see fast results. This type of action orientation is not all bad. How many times have we observed actions taken that, in the short run, would reflect favorably on the area but which, if looked at from a long-run perspective, might have deleterious effects on the area and possibly other areas of the library? Why does that occur? Why should that be allowed to continue? The answer is somewhat simplistic. It is just too difficult to instill an incentive for long-range thinking. Whittaker explains that we do not take the time (or make the time) to go to the next step and look at the real organizational meaning of these actions behind the short-term mentality.[8]

It is the library director's controlling responsibility to ensure that the planning team does not make a habit of creating "quick fix" situations. The "band-aid" approach has to be looked upon with suspicion during the strategic planning process.

Helms reflects the basic philosophy between current performance and future performance:

> According to some fundamental law of nature . . . there is a powerful tendency for all resources to gravitate toward a short-term orientation. The inevitable problems and crises occur, and where do you find the resources to handle them? They always come from the strategic programs, because . . . they are the ones which are postponable. The end result of this process is that, in the absence of restraining forces, after a period of time, all resources are absorbed in short-term activities. This is what happens to the organization which stays so busy that it can never think about the future. It is well down the road toward "playing out its string."[9]

Attitudes Toward Control

As noted earlier, the director cannot delegate the responsibility for the strategic planning process. S/he is the one person on the planning team who has the ultimate control of the planning activity. Naturally, appropriate parts of control can and must be delegated to other members of the planning team. Control is a process that operates through the people in the library. Drucker notes: "One has to realize that even the most powerful "instrument board" complete with computers, operations, research, and simulation, is secondary to the invisible, qualitative control of any human organization, its systems of rewards and punishments, of values and taboos."[10]

The director's attitude toward control is paramount in making the strategic planning system work. In addition to the strong commitment to strategic planning, the director must make it known that s/he wants to take a disciplined approach to the evaluation and control of the strategic planning system. The director's attitude about evaluation and control should be widely known; it will serve as a motivating force for other members of the planning team to develop a similar positive attitude.

REFERENCES

1. William R. King and David I. Cleland, *Strategic Planning and Policy* (New York: Van Nostrand Reinhold, 1978), pp. 349–50.

2. George A. Steiner, "Evaluating Your Strategic Planning System," in *Implementation of Strategic Planning*, Peter Lorange (Englewood Cliffs, NJ: Prentice-Hall, 1982), pp. 36–46.

3. Walter B. Schaffir, *Strategic Business Planning: Some Questions for the Chief Executive* (New York: AMACOM, 1976), pp. 15–16.

4. George A. Steiner, *Strategic Planning: What Every Manager Must Know* (New York: Free Press, 1979), pp. 301–03.

5. Steiner, "Evaluating Your Strategic Planning System," pp. 43–44.

6. John A. Zachman, "Control and Planning of Information Systems," in *The Practice of Planning: Strategic, Administrative, and Operational*, Leon Reinhart et al. (New York: Van Nostrand Reinhold, 1981), p. 285.

7. King and Cleland, p. 357.

8. James B. Whittaker, *Strategic Planning in a Rapidly Changing Environment* (Lexington, MA: Lexington Books, 1978), p. 61.

9. E. W. Helms, "The OST System for Manager Innovation at Texas Instruments" (paper presented to the Armed Forces Management Association, Washington, DC, April 7, 1971).

10. Peter F. Drucker, *Management: Tasks, Responsibilities, Practices* (New York: Harper and Row, 1973), p. 505.

13

CONCLUSION

66 The wise leader considers the days that are yet
to come. 99

—*Persian proverb*

Complex, time-consuming, exciting, systematic, interconnected, action-oriented, long-range, annually recycling, ongoing, and rewarding are some terms used to describe strategic planning. The concept of strategic planning is a powerful one. Strategic planning solely for the sake of having strategic planning is not desirable. To achieve an effective strategic planning system, a library must expend a great deal of effort; the strategic planning process will embrace the entire library.

Bearing in mind the fact that strategy is the most important component of the strategic planning process, the grand design of the planning activity also incorporates the library's mission, goals, objectives, alternatives and contingencies, policies, resource allocation, and an evaluation mechanism. The grand design is enhanced by having a management information system and using principles of the Planning-Programming-Budgeting System. A systematic approach to strategic planning is vital. Budgets and financial plans play an important role as controlling factors. However, they should not overshadow the true strategic aspects of the grand design.

The library's organizational structure will likely be modified by strategy formulation and implementation. Structure will follow strategy. However, the strategic planning system must fit the unique characteristics of a library.

To have an effective strategic planning system, the library must build on its strengths. Managers must know what the strengths are and then develop strategy based upon them. What do we do best? What unique strengths do we have in our collections or in our personnel? Are our strengths the right attributes to fit the opportunities of tomorrow?

Setting goals and objectives is extremely important but not as significant and enduring as choosing strategies. Choosing strategies is the heart of the strategic planning process. The strategy choice process has three primary stages: development, refinement, and evaluation. Development concerns the creation or formulation of strategies that are designed to attain the library's goals and objectives. Refinement refers to reworking and testing strategies so that they reflect the diversity and complexity of the library's goals and objectives. Evaluation is a filtering process in which proposed strategies are closely scrutinized and in which alternative strategies are matched with the goals and objectives. These three stages provide excellent ways of conceptualizing the strategy choice process.

An important function of the planning team is to engage in "backward analysis." That is, the team should identify where the library wants to be in five years, then work back in time from the desired future to the current status. During this regression, it is significant to delineate how the library is to achieve future outcomes at which particular time in the five-year period. By using the "backward analysis" approach, the strategists will determine what pathways (i.e., strategies) have to be used each year from five years hence back to the present year to attain the planned end results. Interdependencies of the goals, objectives, and strategies from one year to the next will be necessary. Strategies used during the five years will be interconnected and dependent on one another. They must not be developed in isolation and cannot function apart from the rest of the library.

The planning process is continuous. It is not necessarily a day-to-day activity, but it has to be given frequent attention. The process is more important than the plan itself. The plan is a closed-end instrument, while the planning process is more sustaining. Once the initial five-year plan is developed, it should be carefully reviewed during each subsequent year. Goals and objectives attained during the first year should be "rolled off" the plan, existing strategies either recycled or discarded. The strategic planning team readapts its thinking and generates new strategies. Thus, the entire library's strategic posture is redefined. Strategic planning requires this type of constant nurturing or it will die or be stillborn.

The real value of strategic planning lies in the thinking it promotes in the library personnel involved with the planning process and its implementation. Participants must think and act strategically. Unquestionably, strategic planning demands more creative thought than any other planning technique.

The planning team realizes other qualitative benefits from the process. Some of the benefits include the following:

- It upgrades management effectiveness through a healthy interchange of ideas and exchanges among members of the team.
- It provides a positive psychological and motivational thrust to the library.
- It helps to strengthen the top managers and ensures their commitment to desired end results.
- It increases the chance of pointing all members of the team in the same direction.
- It helps to achieve better coordination, cooperation, understanding, and integration of collective efforts.

The library director is the chief strategist. This responsibility cannot be delegated nor should it be taken lightly. The director must provide leadership in making strategic planning work effectively.

It is of cardinal importance that the top managers of the library be actively involved with the planning process. They have to provide insight regarding the various areas of the library and display a genuine commitment to the planning endeavor. The excuse that library managers cannot take the time for strategic planning should not be entertained. Moreover, the turbulent environment dictates that the managers must find the requisite time for strategic planning. It is the managers' responsibility to make sure that the process is understood and supported throughout the library.

Strategic planning provides a sound concept for improving the management of the library. Seeing the library's total picture from the perspective of the director is a valuable benefit gleaned by the participants in strategic planning.

Greater attention is now being given to the external environment of the library. In the past, library managers could easily predict the future by extrapolating from past experiences. However, those ''good old days'' are over. The ever-changing external environment stipulates that better planning techniques be employed. A strategic approach to targets of opportunities and potential threats from the external environment is far superior to the thrusts of traditional planning.

Strategic planning requires more than lip service. The ivory tower theorist will never have a successful strategic planning program. The success of strategic planning is not measured by the publication of an impressive, neatly typed "Five-Year Plan." An aspiring plan will not happen merely because it is neatly documented; the library manager must still make it happen. Strategic planning has gained currency as a way to give libraries greater leverage for progress or survival in a changing and unstable world. This, in a nutshell, is the reward for using strategic planning.

SELECTED BIBLIOGRAPHY

Abell, Derek F. "Strategic Windows." *Journal of Marketing* 42 (July 1978): 21–26.

Ackoff, Russell. *A Concept of Corporate Planning*. New York: Wiley-Interscience, 1970.

————. *Creating the Corporate Future: Plan or Be Planned For*. New York: Wiley, 1981.

Albanese, Robert. *Managing: Toward Accountability for Performance*. Homewood, IL: Irwin, 1978.

Anthony, Robert N., and Dearden, John. *Management Control Systems, Text and Cases*. Homewood, IL: Irwin, 1976.

Arcelus, Francisco J., and Schaefer, Norbert V. "Social Demands as Strategic Issues: Some Conceptual Problems." *Strategic Management Journal* 3 (October–December 1982): 347–57.

Argenti, John. *Systematic Corporate Planning*. New York: Halstead Press, 1974.

Armstrong, J. Scott. *Long-Range Forecasting: From Crystal Ball to Computer*. New York: Wiley, 1978.

Arrow, Kenneth J. *The Limits of Organization*. New York: Norton, 1974.

Bales, Carter F. "Strategic Control: The President's Paradox." *Business Horizons* 20 (August 1977): 17–28.

Barmash, Isadore. "Strategic Planning: New Emphasis on Setting Goals and Directions for Retailers: How They Plan." *Stores* 65 (September 1983): 7–9.

Baumol, William J., and Marcus, Matityaha. *Economics of Academic Libraries*. Washington, DC: Council on Education, 1973.

Beckhard, Richard. *Organizational Developments: Strategies and Models*. Reading, MA: Addison-Wesley, 1969.

Behn, Robert D. "Leadership for Cut-Back Management: The Use of a Corporate Strategy." *Journal of Library Administration* 3 (Summer 1982): 89–105.

Bell, Jo Ann, and Keusch, R. B. "Comprehensive Planning for Libraries." *Long Range Planning* 9 (October 1976): 48–56.

Bell, Leslie D. "MIS Strategic Planning." *Infosystems* 29 (May 1982): 32–34.

Belshlov, James A., and Waggener, Herman A. "Keeping the Strategic in Your Strategic Planning." *Management Planning* 28 (March 1980): 23–25.

Benwell, Mary. "Public Participation in Planning—A Research Report." *Long Range Planning* 4 (September 1979): 71–78.

Bermelmans, Thomas. "Strategic Planning for Research and Development." *Long Range Planning* 12 (April 1979): 33–44.

Berry, S. J. "Performance Review: Key to Effective Planning." *Long Range Planning* 12 (December 1979): 17–21.

Bhattacharyya, S. K. *Management Planning and Information Systems.* New Delhi: Learning Systems, 1976.

Brickner, William H., and Cope, Donald M. *The Planning Process.* Cambridge: Winthrop, 1977.

Broholm, Richard R. *Strategic Planning for Church Organizations.* Valley Forge, PA: Judson Press, 1969.

Brown, Maryann Kevin. "Information for Planning." *Journal of Library Administration* 2 (Summer, Fall, Winter 1981): 187–215.

Buijs, J. "Strategic Planning and Product Innovation: Some Systematic Approaches." *Long Range Planning* 12 (October 1979): 23–34.

Burgelman, Robert A. "A Model of the Interaction of Strategic Behavior, Corporate Context, and the Concept of Strategy." *Academy of Management Review* 8 (January 1983): 61–70.

Burgeois, L. J. "Strategy and Environment: A Conceptual Integration." *Academy of Management Review* 5 (January 1980): 25–39.

Burke, W. Warner, and Schmidt, Warren H. "Management and Organization Development: What Is the Target of Change?" *Journal of Library Administration* 1 (Summer 1980): 59–74.

Burns, James MacGregor. *Leadership.* New York: Harper & Row, 1978.

Carlson, Thomas S. "Long-Range Strategic Planning: Is It for Everyone?" *Long Range Planning* 11 (June 1978): 54–61.

Carroll, Peter J. "The Link between Performance and Strategy." *Journal of Business Strategy* 2 (Spring 1982): 3–20.

Chang, Y. N., and Campos-Flores, Fileman. *Business Policy and Strategy.* Santa Monica, CA: Goodyear, 1980.

Cobb, Anthony T., and Marguiles, Newton. "Organizational Development: A Political Perspective." *Management Review* 6 (January 1981): 50–59.

Cohen, Kalman J., and Cyert, Richard M. "Strategy: Formulation, Implementation, and Monitoring." *Journal of Business* 46 (July 1973): 349–67.

Collier, Don. "Strategic Planning Systems Design and Operation." *Journal of Business Strategy* 3 (Summer 1982): 85–89.

Constanin, James A., et al. *Marketing Strategy and Management*. Dallas, TX: Business Publications, 1976.

Cooper, Arnold C., and Schendel, Dan. "Strategic Responses to Technological Threats." *Business Horizons* 19 (February 1976): 61–69.

Corey, E. Raymond, and Star, Stephen H. *Organizational Strategy: A Marketing Approach*. Cambridge, MA: Graduate School of Business Administration, Harvard University, 1970.

Croon, P. C. "Aids in Determining Strategy, the Internal Analysis." *Long Range Planning* 12 (August 1979): 65–73.

Cummings, L. L., and Schwab, Donald P. *Performance in Organizations, Determinants and Appraisal*. Glenview, IL: Scott, Foresman, 1973.

Denning, Basil W. "Strategic Environmental Appraisal." *Long Range Planning* 13 (April 1980): 84–101.

DeProspo, Ernest R. "The Evaluation Component of Planning: An Opinion Essay." *Journal of Library Administration* 2 (Summer, Fall, Winter 1981): 159–72.

Dobbie, John W. "Formal Approaches to Setting Long-Range Goals." *Long Range Planning* 7 (June 1974): 75–81.

Drake, Miriam A. "Managing Innovation in Academic Libraries." *College & Research Libraries* 40 (November 1979): 503–19.

Drucker, Peter. *The New Enterprise*. New York: Harper & Row, 1968.

Easterby-Smith, Mark, and Davies, Julia. "Developing Strategic Thinking: Getting Managers to Contribute Effectively to Strategic Planning." *Long Range Planning* 16 (August 1983): 39–48.

Edinger, Joyce. "Marketing Library Services: Strategy for Survival." *College & Research Libraries* 81 (July 1980): 328–32.

Edmunds, Stahrl W. "The Role of Future Studies in Business Strategic Planning." *Journal of Business Strategy* 3 (Fall 1982): 40–46.

Emshoff, James R., and Finnel, Arthur. "Defining Corporate Strategy: A Case Study Using Strategic Assumptions Analysis." *Sloan Management Review* 20 (Spring 1979): 41–52.

Ewing, David W. *The Human Side of Planning*. New York: Macmillan, 1969.

Ferguson, Charles R. *Measuring Corporate Strategy*. Homewood, IL: Dow Jones-Irwin, 1974.

Filho, Paulo D. V. "Strategic Planning: A New Approach." *Managerial Planning* 30 (March–April 1982): 12–20.

Fischer, David W. "Strategies toward Political Pressures: A Typology of Firm Responses." *Academy of Management Review* 8 (January 1983): 71–78.

Frankenhoff, William P., and Granger, Charles H. "Strategic Management: A New Managerial Concept for an Era of Rapid Change." *Long Range Planning* 3 (April 1971): 7–12.

Galbraith, Jay R., and Nathanson, Daniel A. *Strategy Implementation: The Role of Structure and Process*. New York: West, 1978.

Ghosh, B. C., and Nee, A. Y. C. "Strategic Planning—A Contingency Approach—the Strategic Analysis." *Long Range Planning* 16 (August 1983): 93–103.

Glueck, William F. *Business Policy, Strategy Formulation and Management Action*. 2d ed. New York: McGraw-Hill, 1976.

Goldhaber, Gerald M., et al. *Information Strategies: New Pathways to Corporate Power*. Englewood Cliffs, NJ: Prentice-Hall, 1979.

Gordon, Mitchell. "New Strategy: Planning Research is Counting on It." *Barrons* 62 (April 5, 1982): 44–45.

Grinyer, Peter H., and Yasai-Ardekani, Musoud. "Strategy, Structure, Size and Bureaucracy." *Academy of Management Journal* 24 (September 1981): 471–86.

Gronroos, Christian. "Designing a Long Range Marketing Strategy for Services." *Long Range Planning* 13 (April 1980): 36–42.

Gummesson, Evert. "Organizing for Strategic Management: A Conceptual Model." *Long Range Planning* 12 (October 1979): 62–68.

Gup, Benton E. *Guide to Strategic Planning*. New York: McGraw-Hill, 1980.

Hall, William K. "Survival Strategies in a Hostile Environment." *Harvard Business Review* 58 (September–October 1980): 75–85.

Hammer, Donald P., ed. *The Information Age: Its Development, Its Impact*. Metuchen, NJ: Scarecrow Press, 1976.

Hanson, Ernest I. "The Budgetary Control Function," *The Accounting Review* 23 (April 1966): 239–43.

Heerema, Douglas. "Strategy: The External Challenge." *Business Horizons* (March–April 1981): 2–4.

Hellriegel, Don, and Slochum, John W., eds. *Management: A Contingency Approach*. New York: Addison-Wesley, 1974.

Higgins, J. C. *Strategic and Operational Planning Systems: Principles and Practice*. Englewood Cliffs, NJ: Prentice-Hall, 1980.

Hiller, Robert W. "Role of Finance in Strategic Planning. *Canadian Business Review* 6 (Summer 1979): 22–26.

Hobbs, John M., and Heany, Donald F. "Coupling Strategy to Operating Plans." *Harvard Business Review* 55 (May–June 1977): 119–26.

Hofer, Charles W. "Research on Strategic Planning: A Survey of Past Studies and Suggestions." *Journal of Economics and Business* 28 (Spring–Summer 1976): 261–86.

———. "Toward a Contingency Theory of Business Strategy," *Academy of Management Journal* 18 (December 1975): 784–810.

Hofer, Charles W., and Schendel, Dan. *Strategy Formulation: Analytical Concepts*. St. Paul, MN: West Publishing Co., 1978.

Hollander, Edwin P. *Leadership Dynamics*. New York: The Free Press, 1978.

Holloway, Clark, and King, William R. "Evaluating Alternative Approaches to Strategic Planning." *Long Range Planning* 12 (August 1979): 73–77.

Hopkins, David S. "New Emphasis in Marketing Strategies." *Conference Board Record* 13 (August 1979): 35–39.

House, William C. "Environmental Analysis: Key to More Effective Dynamic Planning." *Managerial Planning* 25 (January–February 1977): 25–29.

Hunsicker, J. Quincy. "The Malaise of Strategic Planning." *Management Review* 69 (March 1980): 9–14.

Irwin, Patrick H. "Changing Organizational Behavior Through Strategic Planning." *Managerial Planning* 23 (September–October 1979): 3–12.

———. "Towards Better Strategic Management." *Long Range Planning* 7 (December 1974): 64–68.

Janzen, L. T. "Systematic Planning and Reorganization." *Long Range Planning* 4 (December 1971): 58–63.

Jauch, Lawrence R., and Osborn, Richard N. "Toward an Integrated Theory of Strategy." *Academy of Management Review* 6 (July 1981): 491–98.

Johnson, Edward R. "Academic Library Planning, Self-Study, and Management Review." *Journal of Library Administration* 2 (Summer, Fall, Winter 1981): 67–79.

Jones, Harry. "Planning and the Chief Executive." *Long Range Planning* 11 (June 1978): 80–84.

Kahalas, Harvey. "A Look at Major Planning Methods: Development, Implementation, Strengths and Limitations." *Long Range Planning* 11 (August 1978): 84–90.

Kantrow, Alan M. "Strategy-Technology Connection." *Harvard Business Review* 58 (July–August 1980): 6–8+.

Kast, Fremont E., and Rosenzweig, James E. *Organization and Management: A Systems Approach*. New York: McGraw-Hill, 1970.

Katz, Gerald, et al. "Strategic Planning in a Restrictive and Competitive Environment: Health Care Institutions." *Health Care Management Review* 8 (Fall 1983): 7–12.

Keller, George. *Academic Strategy: The Management Revolution in American Higher Education*. Baltimore, MD: Johns Hopkins, 1983.

Kemper, Robert E. *Strategic Planning for Library Systems*. D.B.A. diss., University of Washington, 1967.

Kiechel, Walter. "Playing by the Rules of the Corporate Strategy Game." *Fortune 100* (September 24, 1979): 110–12+.

Klein, Walter H., and Murphy, David C. *Policy Concepts in Organizational Guidance*. Boston: Little, Brown, 1973.

Kloeze, H. J., et al. "Strategic Planning and Participation: A Contradiction in Terms?" *Long Range Planning* 13 (October 1980): 10–20.

Koontz, Harold. "Making Strategic Planning Work." *Business Horizons* 19 (April 1976): 37–47.

Kotler, Philip. *Marketing for Nonprofit Organizations*. Englewood Cliffs: NJ: Prentice-Hall, 1975.

Kotter, John P., and Schlesinger, Leonard A. "Choosing Strategies for Change." *Harvard Business Review* 57 (March–April 1979): 106–14.

Krane, Robert A. "Let's Plan Our Future, Not Stumble into It." *ABA Banking Journal* 75 (July 1983): 43+.

Kudla, Ronald J. "The Components of Strategic Planning." *Long Range Planning* 11 (December 1978): 48–52.

Lentz, R. T. "Strategic Capability: A Concept and Framework for Analysis." *Academy of Management Review* 5 (April 1980): 225–34.

Leone, Robert A., and Meyer, John R. "Capacity Strategies for the 1980s." *Harvard Business Review* 58 (November–December 1980): 133–40.

Leontiades, Milton. "Choosing the Right Manager to Fit the Strategy." *Journal of Business Strategy* 3 (Fall 1982): 58–69.

Liesener, James W. "Systematic Planning in School Library Media Programs." *Journal of Library Administration* 2 (Summer, Fall, Winter 1981): 97–112.

Litecky, Charles R. "Corporate Strategy and MIS Planning." *Journal of Systems Management* 32 (January 1981): 36–39.

Londoner, Caroll A. "The Systems Approach as an Administrative and Program Planning Tool for Continuing Education." *Educational Technology* 12 (August 1972): 24–31.

Lorange, Peter. *Implementation of Strategic Planning*. Englewood Cliffs, NJ: Prentice-Hall, 1982.

Lorange, Peter, and Vancil, Richard F. "How to Design a Strategic Planning System." *Harvard Business Review* 54 (September 1976): 75–81.

————. *Strategic Planning Systems*. Englewood Cliffs, NJ: Prentice-Hall, 1977.

Luck, David J., and Ferrell, O. E. *Marketing Strategy and Plans, Systematic Marketing Management*. Englewood Cliffs, NJ: Prentice-Hall, 1979.

McCarthy, Daniel J., et al. *Business Policy and Strategy: Concepts and Readings*. Homewood, IL: Irwin, 1979.

McClure, Charles R. *Information for Academic Library Decision Making: The Case for Organization Information Management*. Westport, CT: Greenwood Press, 1980.

————. "Planning for Library Effectiveness: The Role of Information Resources Management." *Journal of Library Administration* 1 (Fall 1980): 3–32.

McClure, Charles R., and Hill, Linda L. "Special Considerations for Corporate Library Planning: Moving toward Information Resources Management." *Journal of Library Administration* 2 (Summer, Fall, Winter, 1981): 113–28.

Maciariello, Joseph A. *Program-Management Control Systems*. New York: Wiley, 1978.

McKay, Charles W., and Cutting, Guy D. "A Model for Long Range Planning in Higher Education." *Long Range Planning* 7 (October 1974): 58–60.

McNichols, Thomas J. *Executive Policy and Strategic Planning*. New York: McGraw-Hill, 1977.

Martin, Allie Beth. *A Strategy for Public Library Change*. Chicago: American Library Association, 1972.

Mazzolini, Renato. "How Strategic Decisions Are Made." *Long Range Planning* 14 (June 1981): 85–96.

Meares, Carol Ann. "Strategies for Survival: Succeeding in the Decades of Change." *Management World* 12 (January 1983): 1+.

Menke, Michael. "Strategic Planning in an Age of Uncertainty." *Long Range Planning* 12 (August 1979): 27–34.

Merson, John C., and Qualls, Robert L. *Strategic Planning for Colleges and Universities: A Systems Approach to Planning and Resource Allocation*. San Antonio, TX: Trinity University Press, 1979.

Michael, S. R. "Guidelines for Contingency Approach to Planning." *Long Range Planning* 12 (December 1979): 62–69.

Miles, Raymond E., and Snow, Charles C. *Organizational Strategy, Structure, and Process*. New York: McGraw-Hill, 1978.

Miller, Danny, and Friesen, Peter H. "Archetypes of Strategy Formulation." *Management Science* 24 (May 1978): 921–33.

Mingle, James R. *Challenges of Retrenchment: Strategies for Consolidating Programs, Cutting Costs, and Reallocating Resources*. San Francisco, CA: Jossey-Bass, 1981.

Mintzberg, Henry. "The Manager's Job: Folklore and Fact." *Harvard Business Review* 53 (July–August 1975): 49–61.

―――. *The Nature of Managerial Work*. New York: Harper & Row, 1973.

Mintzburg, Henry, and Waters, James A. "Tracking Strategy in an Entrepreneurial Firm." *Academy of Management Journal* 25 (September 1982): 465–99.

Mitchell, Donald W. "Pursuing Strategic Potential." *Managerial Planning* 28 (May–June 1980): 6–10.

Montgomery, David B., and Weinberg, Charles B. "Toward Strategic Intelligence Systems." *Journal of Marketing* 43 (Fall 1979): 41–52.

Morton, Maxwell R. "Technology and Strategy: Creating a Successful Partnership." *Business Horizons* 26 (January–February 1983): 44–48.

Moskow, Michael H. *Strategic Planning in Business and Government*. New York: Committee for Economic Development, 1978.

Murray, M. A. "Comparing Public and Private Management: An Exploratory Essay." *Public Administration Review* 35 (July 1975):364–71.

Nair, Keshavan, and Sarin, Rakesh K. "Generating Future Scenarios—Their Use in Strategic Planning." *Long Range Planning* 12 (June 1974): 23–32.

Nash, Thomas. "Organizing for Strategic Planning." *Managerial Planning* 28 (July–August 1979): 3–9.

Naylor, Thomas H. *Optimization Models for Strategic Planning*. New York: Elsevier Science Publishing Co., 1984.

―――. "The Strategy Matrix." *Managerial Planning* 31 (January–February 1983): 4–9.

Neubauer, F. Friedrich, and Solomon, Norman B. "A Managerial Approach to Environmental Assessment." *Long Range Planning* 10 (April 1977): 14–20.

Newman, William H. "Shaping the Master Strategy of Your Firm." *California Management Review* 9 (Spring 1967): 77–88.

Newman, William H., and Wallender, Harvey W. "Managing Not-for-Profit Enterprises." *Journal of Library Administration* 1 (Spring 1980): 87–97.

Ohmae, Kenichi. "Foresight in Strategic Planning: Excerpt from the Mind of the Strategist." *McKinsey Quarterly* (Autumn 1982): 14–31.

———. "The Secret of Strategic Vision." *Management Review* 71 (April 1982): 9–13.

Oldman, Christine. "Marketing Library and Information Services." *European Journal of Marketing* 11 (Spring 1977): 460–74.

Orr, R. H. "Measuring the Goodness of Library Services: A General Framework for Considering Quantitative Measures." *Journal of Documentation* 29 (September 1973): 315–33.

Osmond, C. N. "Corporate Planning: Its Impact on Management." *Long Range Planning* 3 (April 1971): 34–40.

Owen, Arthur A. "How to Implement Strategy." *Management Today* (July 1982): 50–53+.

Paine, Frank T., and Naumes, William. *Organizational Strategy and Policy: Text Cases and Incidents*. Philadelphia, PA: W. B. Saunders Co., 1975.

Pascarella, Perry. "Is Your Mission Clear?" *Industry Week* 219 (November 14, 1983): 75–76.

———. "The Uphill Battle to Think Strategically." *Industry Week* 218 (September 19, 1983): 73+.

Paulson, Robert D. "Chief Executive As Change Agent." *Management Review* 71 (February 1982): 25–28+.

Perham, John. "Strategic Planners Take Over." *Duns Review* 115 (June 1980): 72–73+.

Peters, Thomas J., and Waterman, Robert H. *In Search of Excellence: Lessons from America's Best-Run Companies*. New York: Warner Books, 1982.

Pings, Vern M. "Use or Value of Goals and Objectives Statements." *Journal of Library Administration* 1 (Fall 1980): 55–62.

Porter, Michael E. "How Competititve Forces Shape Strategy." *Harvard Business Review* 57 (March–April 1979): 137–45.

Quinn, James B. "Managing Strategic Change." *Sloan Management Review* 21 (Summer 1980): 3–20.

Quinn, James Brian. "Strategic Goals: Process and Politics." *Sloan Management Review* 19 (Fall 1977): 21–37.

Reimnitz, Charles A. "Testing a Planning and Control Model in Nonprofit Organizations." *Academy of Management Journal* 15 (March 1972): 77–87.

Richards, Max D. *Organizational Goal Structures*. St. Paul, MN: West Publishing Co., 1978.

Rossi, Peter H., et al. *Evaluation: A Systematic Approach*. Beverly Hills, CA: Sage Publications, 1980.

Rothschild, William E. *Putting It All Together: A Guide to Strategic Thinking*. New York: American Management Association, 1976.

Ruggles, Rudy L. "Developing Systems for Strategic Planning." *Long Range Planning* 3 (June 1971): 39–43.

Schellenberger, Robert, and Boseman, Glen F. *Policy Formulation and Strategy Management*. New York: Wiley, 1978.

Schendel, Dan, et al. "Corporate Turnaround Strategies." *Journal of General Management* 3 (Spring 1976): 3–11.

Schleh, Edward C. "Strategic Planning: No Sure Cure for Corporate Surprises." *Management Review* 68 (March 1979): 54–57.

Shah, Kiran, and LaPlaca, Peter J. "Assessing Risks in Strategic Planning." *Industrial Marketing Management* 10 (April 1981): 77–91.

Shanklin, William L. "Strategic Business Planning: Yesterday, Today and Tomorrow." *Business Horizons* 22 (October 1979): 7–14.

Shapiro, Irving S. "Today's Executive: Private Steward and Public Servant." *Harvard Business Review* 56 (March–April 1978): 94–101.

Shirley, Robert, et al. *Strategy and Policy Formulation: A Multifunctional Orientation*. New York: Wiley, 1976.

Shuman, Jack N. "Strategic Planning and Information Systems." *ASIS Bulletin* 8 (June 1982): 23–27.

Slatter, Stuart St. P. "Strategic Planning for Public Relations." *Long Range Planning* 13 (June 1980): 57–60.

Smith, Eddie C. "Strategic Business Planning and Human Resources." *Personnel Journal* 61 (August 1982): 606–10.

Smith, Ward C. "Product Life-Cycle Strategy: How to Stay on the Growth Curve." *Management Review* 69 (January 1980): 8–13.

Snow, Charles C., and Hrebiniak, Lawrence. "Strategy, Distinctive Competence, and Organizational Performance." *Administrative Science Quarterly* 25 (June 1980): 317–36.

Steers, Richard M. *Organizational Effectiveness, A Behavior View*. Santa Monica, CA: Goodyear, 1977.

Steiner, George A., and Miner, John B. *Management Policy and Strategy*. New York: Macmillan, 1977.

Stonich, Paul J., and Wernecke, Susan Graham. "Strategy Formulation: What to Avoid; How to Succeed." *Management Review* 71 (May 1982): 25–28+.

Taylor, Bernard. "Strategies for Planning." *Long Range Planning* 8 (August 1975): 27–40.

Taylor, Bernard, and Sparkes, John R. *Corporate Strategy and Planning*. New York: Wiley, 1977.

Taylor, Derek E. "Strategic Planning As an Organizational Change Process: Some Guidelines from Practice." *Long Range Planning* 12 (October 1979): 45–53.

Thune, Stanley, and House, Robert J. "Where Long Range Planning Pays Off." *Business Horizons* 8 (August 1970): 81–87.

Tilles, Seymour. "The Manager's Job: A Systems Approach." *Harvard Business Review* 41 (January–February 1963): 73–81.

Toll, John S. "Strategic Planning: An Increasing Priority for Colleges and Universities." *Change* 14 (May–June 1982): 36–37.

Travernier, Gerard. "Changing Climate for Future Managers." *International Management* 31 (August 1976): 10–14.

Tregoe, Benjamin B., and Zimmerman, John W. "Strategic Thinking: Key to Corporate Survival." *Management Review* 68 (February 1979): 9–14.

Tricker, R. I. "How to Plan Information Strategy." *Management Today* (September 1982): 62–65+.

Uyterhoeven, Hugo E. R., et al. *Strategy and Organization: Text and Cases in General Management*. Homewood, IL: Irwin, 1977.

Van Hoorn, T. P. "Strategic Planning in Small and Medium-Sized Companies." *Long Range Planning* 12 (April 1979): 84–91.

Van Kirk, John E., and Noonan, Kathleen. "Key Factors in Strategic Planning." *Journal of Small Business Management* 20 (July 1982): 1–7.

Vance, Jack O. "The Anatomy of a Corporate Strategy." *California Management Review* 13 (Fall 1970): 5–12.

———. "The Accuracy of Long-Range Planning." *Harvard Business Review* 48 (September–October 1970): 98–101.

Vancil, Richard F. "The Accuracy of Long-Range Planning." *Harvard Business Review* 48 (September–October 1970): 98–101.

———. "Strategy Formulation in Complex Organizations." *Sloan Management Review* 54 (Winter 1976): 32–41.

Vesper, V. D. "Strategic Mapping—A Tool for Corporate Planners." *Long Range Planning* 12 (December 1979): 75–92.

Ward, E. Peter. *The Dynamics of Planning*. New York: Pergamon Press, 1970.

Ward, Lane D. "Eight Steps to Strategic Planning for Training Managers." *Training* 19 (November 1982): 22–23+.

Wasserman, Paul, and Ford, Gary T. "Marketing and Marketing Research: What the Library Manager Should Learn." *Journal of Library Administration* 1 (Spring 1980): 19–29.

Weingand, Darlene E. "The Janus Syndrome: Guarding the Library Gates in a Time of Economic Need." *Journal of Library Administration* 3 (Summer 1982): 51–59.

Weir, G. A. "Developing Strategies: A Practical Approach." *Long Range Planning* 7 (October 1974): 7–12.

White, Herbert S. *Managing the Special Library: Strategies for Success Within the Larger Organization*. White Plains, NY: Knowledge Industry, 1984.

Wood, Elizabeth J. "Strategic Planning and the Marketing Process: Library Applications." *Journal of Academic Librarianship* 9 (March 1983): 15–20.

Woodward, Herbert N. "Management Strategies for Small Companies." *Harvard Business Review* 54 (January–February 1976): 113–21.

Young, R. Clifton. "Strategic Overview of Business Information Systems." *Managerial Planning* 29 (March–April 1981): 28–37.

INDEX